Understanding
Developmental
Dyspraxia

A Textbook for Students and Professionals

Madeleine Portwood

David Fulton Publishers
London

David Fulton Publishers Ltd
Ormond House, 26–27 Boswell Street, London WC1N 3JZ

www.fultonpublishers.co.uk

First published in Great Britain by David Fulton Publishers 2000
Reprinted 2000, 2001

Note: The right of Madeleine Portwood to be identified as the author of this work has been asserted by her in accordance with the Copyright, Designs and Patents Act 1988.

British Library Cataloguing in Publication Data
A catalogue record for this book is available from the British Library

ISBN 1–85346–574–7

Typeset by Elite Typesetting Techniques, Eastleigh, Hampshire
Printed in Great Britain by The Cromwell Press Ltd, Trowbridge, Wilts.

Contents

Foreword

Dyspraxia is a serious condition affecting perhaps six per cent of children and causing significant distress and educational difficulty.

As a parent of a child who has both developmental dyspraxia and attention deficit hyperactivity disorder, I have been very aware of the issues of comorbidity and of the difficulties in obtaining an appropriate diagnosis. As a professional working with children and adults with learning disability, many of whom have other disorders including developmental dyspraxia, I am aware of the difficulty of making the right diagnosis and finding the right services for affected individuals.

I am therefore delighted to welcome this book and commend it to professionals and parents alike. It gives a lucid, accessible and comprehensive account of current knowledge of the aetiology and presentation of dyspraxia and of related difficulties. It provides very helpful advice on appropriate assessment, relevant legal issues and useful intervention.

Madeleine Portwood has been working in a professional and voluntary capacity, helping children and adults with dyspraxia for some ten years. She brings to this work her wealth of experience in the field and a detailed knowledge of current research issues. This is the only book of which I am aware that covers these issues in such detail and I am sure it will become a valued textbook in the field.

Dr Jane Radley
Consultant Psychiatrist
Northgate Hospital, Morpeth
January 2000

Preface

Since the publication of my first text on developmental dyspraxia in 1996 there has been extensive research into the origins, diagnosis and treatment of the disorder. The purpose of this volume is to provide a handbook for clinicians that considers not only the characteristics of dyspraxia but also the comorbidity of other developmental disorders: attention-deficit hyperactivity disorder, autistic spectrum disorders and dyslexia.

There is further discussion on the validity of neuropsychometric assessment when 'profiles', apparently characterising dyspraxia, show marked similarities to those of youngsters with identified syndromes: Turners, Williams and Smith-Magensis. As a result of this increasing awareness among professionals, many of the children not previously diagnosed with these specific conditions are now identified.

Assessment must consider all aspects of development to ensure that an accurate diagnosis is made and attention is not focused solely on the 'primary' presenting disorder. The research cited in chapter one suggests that the comorbidity of developmental disorders is as high as 40 per cent and in such cases the provision made should consider all of the presenting difficulties.

In my work during the past ten years I have become increasingly aware of the difficulties and frustration experienced by children and their families who move between professionals in an attempt to obtain a diagnosis. The struggle continues as the families attempt to gain access to appropriate services. Early identification would have a significant effect on future outcomes and raised awareness amongst professionals involved with young children, in particular health visitors and adults working with pre-schoolers in playgroups or nurseries is important.

I have offered some discussion on the roles of the Health and Education Authorities in identifying and making provision for such youngsters. Perhaps it would not be too difficult to provide training for the educators of the future in colleges of education or students in disciplines such as medicine, psychology, optometry, physio/occupational therapy, speech therapy and nursing.

I believe that there is a wealth of experience and support already available but it is necessary to co-ordinate these services and ensure that systems are in place to make them accessible for children and adults alike.

Madeleine Portwood
Durham, January 2000

Acknowledgements

I would like to extend my thanks to the children and parents who have contributed to my research and allowed their case studies to be presented. In addition, I am grateful to the adults who have given me some insight into the difficulties experienced when identification and support has not been made available in childhood.

I have benefited from the support of my professional colleagues, in particular the Principal Educational Psychologist for Durham, David Smith, and the Director of Education, Keith Mitchell.

I am also grateful to the following who, through their particular specialisms and involvement with youngsters, have provided invaluable supplementary material:

- The staff and pupils at Elemore Hall School; in particular Mike Davey, Headmaster, Lynn Gibson, Specialist Senior Educational Psychologist (Durham E.P.S.), Barbara Barron and Joan Huntingdon, Support Staff and Chris Ridley, Project Co-ordinator.
- Alan Duff, Advisory Teacher in Physical Education
- Dave Ford, Senior Primary Inspector and Janet Bennett, Early Years Inspection Officer, who produced the Durham Scheme for Baseline Assessment 'Flying Start'.

Finally, I thank those who have been directly involved in the production of this text:

- John O'Neill and Joanne Clark – illustrations
- Gillian Bell – additional research
- John Portwood – data analysis
- Peter Chislett and Sally Critchlow – editing and proof reading.

Chapter 1

Defining dyspraxia

The purpose of this text is to provide clinicians with current research information and facilitate the diagnosis of developmental dyspraxia. The most appropriate starting point is to consider the acknowledged diagnostic criteria in the Manual of the American Psychiatric Association.

Dyspraxia is a developmental condition and the comorbidity with autistic spectrum disorders, dyslexia and 'Attention Deficit and Hyperactivity Disorder' (ADHD) is high. My own research between 1988 and 1999 (Portwood 1999) suggests that it is probably between 40 per cent and 45 per cent.

Szatmari *et al.* (1989a) state that the comorbidity of ADHD with other disorders is common with up to 44 per cent of those identified having at least one other condition and 32 per cent having two or more.

Barkley (1990) comparing ADHD children with controls found they were considerably more likely to display associated problems with academic achievement, language and motor co-ordination, as many as 25 per cent having significant delays in the development of maths, reading or spelling and up to 30 per cent showing problems with language.

In addition, parents of ADHD children described their youngsters as being less co-ordinated than expected for their age.

The overlap between dyspraxia, ADHD, and other developmental disorders is evident when comparing the descriptions contained in the American Psychiatric Association Diagnostic and Statistical Manual (DSM-IV 1994). An overview is essential before attempting to determine which conditions are present.

'**Learning Disorders**' describes specific difficulties in reading (dyslexia), mathematics and handwriting.

'**Developmental Co-ordination Disorder** (DCD)' identifies as its essential feature a marked impairment in the development of motor co-ordination (dyspraxia).

Diagnostic features of Developmental Co-ordination Disorder (315.4)

The essential feature of Developmental Co-ordination Disorder is a marked impairment in the development of motor co-ordination (Criterion A). The diagnosis is made only if this impairment significantly interferes with academic achievement or activities of daily living (Criterion B). The diagnosis is made if the co-ordination difficulties are not due to a general medical condition (e.g., cerebral palsy, hemiplegia, or muscular dystrophy) and the criteria are not met for Pervasive Developmental Disorder (Criterion C). If Mental Retardation is present, the motor difficulties are in excess of those usually associated with it (Criterion D). The manifestations of this disorder vary with age and development. For example, younger children may display clumsiness and delays in achieving development motor milestones (e.g., walking, crawling, sitting, tying shoelaces, buttoning shirts, zipping trousers). Older children may display difficulties with the motor aspects of assembling puzzles, building models, playing ball, and printing or writing.

Associated features and disorders

Problems commonly associated with Developmental Co-ordination Disorder include delays in other non-motor milestones. Associated disorders may include Phonological Disorder, Expressive Language Disorder, and Mixed Receptive-Expressive Language Disorder. Prevalence of Developmental Co-ordination Disorder has been estimated to be as high as 6 per cent for children in the age range of 5–11 years. Recognition of Developmental Co-ordination Disorder usually occurs when the child first attempts such tasks as running, holding a knife and fork, buttoning clothes, or playing ball games. Its progression is variable. In some cases, lack of co-ordination continues through adolescence and adulthood.

Differential diagnosis

Developmental Co-ordination Disorder must be distinguished from motor impairments that are due to a general medical condition. Problems in co-ordination may be associated with specific neurological disorders (e.g., cerebral palsy, progressive lesions of the cerebellum), but in these cases there is definite neural damage and abnormal findings on neurological examination. If Mental Retardation is present, Developmental Co-ordination Disorder can be diagnosed only if the motor difficulties are in excess of those usually associated with the Mental Retardation. A diagnosis of Developmental Co-ordination Disorder is not given if the criteria are met for a Pervasive Developmental Disorder. Individuals with Attention Deficit Hyperactivity Disorder may fall, bump into things, or knock things over, but this is usually due to distractibility and impulsiveness rather than to a motor impairment. If criteria for both disorders are met, both diagnoses can be given.

Summary of diagnostic criteria for Developmental Co-ordination Disorder (315.4)

A. Performance in daily activities which require motor co-ordination is substantially below that expected given the person's chronological age and measured intelligence. This may be manifested by marked delays in achieving motor milestones (e.g., walking, crawling, sitting), dropping things, 'clumsiness', poor performance in sports, or poor handwriting.

B. The disturbance in Criterion A significantly interferes with academic achievement or activities of daily living.

C. The disturbance is not due to a general medical condition (e.g. cerebral palsy, hemiplegia, or muscular dystrophy) and does not meet criteria for a Pervasive Developmental Disorder.

D. If Mental Retardation is present, the motor difficulties are in excess of those usually associated with it.

Criteria for Attention Deficit Hyperactivity Disorder (ADHD) (314.01)

A. Either (1) or (2):

(1) Inattention: at least **six** of the following symptoms of inattention have persisted for at least six months to a degree that is maladaptive and inconsistent with developmental level:

(a) often fails to give close attention to details or makes careless mistakes in schoolwork, work, or other activities
(b) often has difficulty sustaining attention in tasks or play activities
(c) often does not seem to listen to what is being said to him/her
(d) often does not follow through on instructions and fails to finish schoolwork, chores, or duties in the workplace (not due to oppositional behaviour or failure to understand instructions)
(e) often has difficulties organising tasks and activities
(f) often avoids or strongly dislikes tasks (such as schoolwork or homework) that require sustained mental effort
(g) often loses things necessary for tasks or activities (e.g., school assignments, pencils, books, tools, or toys)
(h) often easily distracted by extraneous stimuli
(i) often forgetful in daily activities.

(2) Hyperactivity – Impulsivity: at least **four** of the following symptoms of hyperactivity – impulsivity have persisted for at least six months to a degree that is maladaptive and inconsistent with developmental level:

(a) often fidgets with hands or feet or squirms in seat
(b) leaves seat in classroom or in other situations in which remaining seated is expected
(c) often runs about or climbs excessively in situations where it is inappropriate (in adolescents or adults, may be limited to subjective feelings of restlessness)
(d) often has difficulty playing or engaging in leisure activities quietly.
(e) often blurts out answers to questions before the questions have been completed

(f) often has difficulty waiting in lines or awaiting turn in games or group situations.

B. Onset no later than age seven.

C. Symptoms must be present in two or more situations (e.g. at school, work, and at home).

D. The disturbance causes clinically significant distress or impairment in social, academic, or occupational functioning.

E. Does not occur exclusively during the course of PDD, Schizophrenia or other Psychotic Disorder, and is not better accounted for by Mood, Anxiety, Dissociative, or Personality Disorder.

Criteria for Autism Disorder (299.00)

A. A total of six (or more) items from (1), (2) and (3), with at least two from (1), and one each from (2) and (3).

(1) Qualitative impairment in social interaction, as manifested by at least two of the following:

(a) marked impairments in the use of multiple non-verbal behaviours such as eye-to-eye gaze, facial expression, body posture, and gestures to regulate social interaction

(b) failure to develop peer relationships appropriate to developmental level

(c) lack of spontaneous seeking to share enjoyment, interests, or achievements with other people, (e.g., by a lack of showing, bringing, or pointing out objects of interest to other people)

(d) lack of social or emotional reciprocity (note: in the description, it gives the following as examples: not actively participating in simple social play or games, preferring solitary activities, or involving others in activities only as tools or 'mechanical' aids).

(2) Qualitative impairments in communication as manifested by at least one of the following:

(a) delay in or total lack of the development of spoken language (not accompanied by an attempt to compensate through alternative modes of communication such as gesture or mime)

(b) in individuals with adequate speech, marked impairment in the ability to initiate or sustain a conversation with others

(c) stereotyped and repetitive use of language or idiosyncratic language

(d) lack of varied, spontaneous make-believe play or social imitative play appropriate to developmental level.

(3) Restricted, repetitive and stereotyped patterns of behaviour, interests and activities, as manifested by at least two of the following:

(a) encompassing preoccupation with one or more stereotyped and restricted patterns of interest that is abnormal either in intensity or focus

(b) apparently inflexible adherence to specific, non-functional routines or rituals

(c) stereotyped and repetitive motor mannerisms (e.g. hand or finger flapping or twisting, or complex whole-body movements)

(d) persistent preoccupation with parts of objects.

B. Delays or abnormal functioning in at least one of the following areas, with onset prior to age three years:

1. Social interaction
2. Language as used in social communication
3. Symbolic or imaginative play.

C. The disturbance is not better accounted for by Rett's Disorder or Childhood Disintegrative Disorder.

Criteria for diagnosis of Asperger's Disorder (299.80)

- At least two demonstrations of impaired social interaction. The patient:
  - Shows a marked inability to regulate social interaction by using multiple non-verbal behaviours such as body posture and gestures, eye contact and facial expression.
  - Doesn't develop peer relationships that are appropriate to the developmental level.
  - Doesn't seek to share achievements, interests or pleasure with others.
  - Lacks social or emotional reciprocity.
- Activities, behaviour and interests that are repetitive, restricted and stereotyped (at least one of):
  - Preoccupation with abnormal (in focus or intensity) interests that are restricted and stereotyped (such as spinning things).
  - Rigidly sticks to routines or rituals that don't appear to have a function.
  - Has stereotyped, repetitive motor mannerisms (such as hand flapping).
  - Persistently preoccupied with parts of objects.
- The symptoms cause clinically important impairment in social, occupational or personal functioning.
- There is no clinically important general language delay (the child can speak words by age two, phrases by age three).
- There is no clinically important delay in developing cognition, age-appropriate self-help skills, adaptive behaviour (except social interaction) and normal curiosity about the environment.
- The patient doesn't fulfil criteria for schizophrenia or another specific Pervasive Developmental Disorder.

Learning Disorders (315.00)

Reading disorder

- As measured by a standardised test that is given individually, the patient's ability to read (accuracy or comprehension) is substantially less than would be expected considering age, intelligence and education.

- This deficiency materially impedes academic achievement or daily living.
- If there is also a sensory defect, the reading deficiency is worse than would be expected with it.

Mathematics disorder

- As measured by a standardised test that is given individually, the patient's mathematical ability is substantially less than would be expected considering age, intelligence and education.
- This deficiency materially impedes academic achievement or daily living.
- If there is also a sensory defect, the mathematics deficiency is worse than would be expected with it.

Disorder of written expression

- As measured by functional assessment or by a standardised test that is given individually, the patient's writing ability is substantially less than would be expected considering age, intelligence and education.
- The difficulty with writing grammatically correct sentences and organised paragraphs materially impedes academic achievement or daily living.
- If there is also a sensory defect, the writing deficiency is worse than would be expected with it.

Related Specific Developmental Disorders

The Diagnostic and Statistical Manual refers to the different learning disorders (LD) as Specific Developmental Disorders. They are identified as particular academic skill areas which have failed to develop as expected given the child's intellectual ability and educational experience. In addition to these Specific Developmental Disorders in arithmetic, writing and reading, several disorders of speech and language are also defined: Developmental Articulation Disorder, Developmental Expressive Language Disorder and Developmental Receptive Language Disorder.

'Diagnosis' of a condition is often dependent on the route of the referral. If a particular outcome is expected, it is possible to 'select' the symptoms most indicative of that disorder. Checklists are notoriously good at facilitating this method of assessment. It is insufficient to observe the child's presenting behaviours without obtaining a developmental history and undertaking a detailed assessment. Too often the 'primary' presenting difficulty is identified and supported while the underlying causes remain 'untreated'. It is not enough for the clinician to know the criteria for the diagnosis of dyspraxia or ADHD; he/she must be able to distinguish the presenting symptoms from the other conditions which have similar characteristics.

Case study

A six year old boy presents as having difficulty with the articulation of speech. There is no evidence of a receptive language problem. Father and elder brother have a history of delayed language acquisition. There was also some delay in the development of motor co-ordination and perceptual skills.

With such information, it could be assumed that here is a 'classic' case of dyspraxia. My own research (1999) identified delayed acquisition of speech in 45 per cent of the identified sample population. However, consideration should be given to the following studies.

Szatmari *et al.* (1989b) and Barkley (1990) agree that between 10 and 54 per cent of the children with ADHD have problems with expressive, but not receptive, language compared with 2 to 25 per cent in the control groups. ADHD children will probably say more in conversation than the controls (Zentall 1988) although when confronted with tasks which require specific verbal responses they are likely to be much more dysfluent.

Hartsough and Lambert (1985) identified more than 50 per cent of a sample of ADHD children as having poor motor co-ordination with Shaywitz and Shaywitz (1984) finding a high percentage of ADHD youngsters with perceptual difficulties.

To move towards an accurate diagnosis Barkley (1990) states:

> the clinician brings to the case the wealth of previous clinical and research literature that has accumulated on groups of children with the same diagnosis. This literature may then point the way to other treatments and information about the course and outcome of the disorder, and to potential aetiologies of it.

The chapters which follow are intended to provide such additional information with regard to the neurological principles of dyspraxia, factors influencing early development and the role of professionals in diagnosing the condition.

Chapter 2

Dyspraxia: the neurological basis

The brain is responsible for monitoring and adapting the body's reaction to the environment. It also mediates processes such as thought, perception, language and emotion as well as fine and gross motor skills. The vast majority of developmental disorders of childhood are attributable to some 'brain-related' event. It is important to have an understanding of the neurological processes to apply this knowledge when undertaking the assessment of children.

At birth the infant brain has its full complement of neurones (nerve cells). Unlike most organs of the body, whose cells divide and die in a matter of weeks, brain cells continue for the lifetime of the organism. The structural development of the brain is a lifelong process as connections between the nerve cells become more complex.

The neurone

The neurone is the fundamental building block of the brain's structure. The brain comprises approximately 10 billion neurones and their most important feature is an ability to actively make and break connections with other neurones – in some cases up to as many as 10,000; in others only 1 or 2 in neural networks. It is the process of forming these neural networks which gives the brain the capacity to learn (Figure 2.1).

The major feature of the neurone is the axon leading from the cell which is covered in a myelin sheath. It is through the axon that an electrical pulse can travel through the brain. At the end of the axon there is a gap – the synapse – which is the point at which the message is transferred from one cell to the next. It is a specialised structure in which electrical activity passed down the axon of the transmitting neurone leads to the release of a chemical (a neurotransmitter) which in turn induces electrical activity in the receiving neurone. As a result, nerve signals in the form of electrical discharges occur at the membranes of the neurones. The synaptic junction is where the signal transfer takes place and the neurone discharges or 'fires' when it is stimulated to a specific threshold. The neurone's sensitivity to stimulation can be altered by a variety of different chemicals, including the neurotransmitters at synapses and also drugs (Figure 2.2).

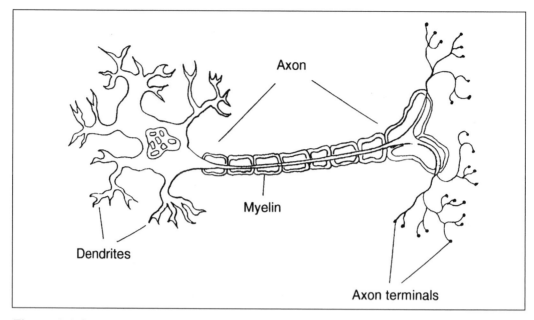

Figure 2.1 Structure of a neurone

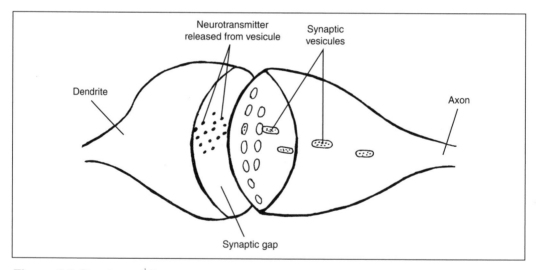

Figure 2.2 Structure of the synapse

The dendrites are the 'receivers' of the information transmitted from the axons of other nerve cells and they usually transfer sensory information towards the central nervous system.

It is not normally the case that an electrical signal travels directly as the result of one neurone firing an electrical pulse to another. Some nerve cells have as many as half a million dendrites receiving impulses from other cells. A threshold level of excitability is required and this threshold is usually reached when several different nerve cells are fired towards the same receiving nerve cell. It is only then that the recipient cell will respond. This is described as an 'all or nothing' response.

Neurones do not wait long periods before 'firing'. Many regularly fire ten times per second. It appears that it is the pattern of firing neurones which is important. This process involves the physical transfer of matter – the neurotransmitter, which is produced and contained in a synaptic vesicle before release. Furthermore, this process requires energy which is supplied by mitochondria found in the cell. As a consequence, the nerve cell requires a constant supply of material to replace that which is lost. These materials found in the synapse itself must be sufficient to enable the passage of the neurotransmitter.

It is appropriate at this stage to discuss in more detail the nutritional requirements for the neurotransmitter which enable it to carry out its function appropriately. The brain comprises 60 per cent fat, 25 per cent of which is a single substance: docosahexanoic acid (DHA). Fat is one of the three main constituents of food, the others being carbohydrate and protein, and is the primary means by which energy is stored in the body. In addition there are substances called 'fatty acids' which are the key structural elements to the cell membranes in the body. Although there are many different types of fatty acids it is the long chain polyunsaturated fatty acids (LCPUFAs or LCPs) which have been the focus of much research.

In terms of human nutrition the two most significant types of these unsaturated fatty acids are Omega-6 and Omega-3. The two most important polyunsaturated Omega-3 acids are eicosapentaenoic acid (EPA) and docosahexanoic acid (DHA). The most important Omega-6 fatty acid is arachidonic acid (ARA). Omega-6 fatty acids are found predominantly in commercial plant and animal food sources while Omega-3 fatty acids are found in highest quantities in marine fish and algae.

Omega-6 and Omega-3 fatty acids have different biological roles in the body and compete for certain enzymes to perform their respective functions and therefore balance between the two is vital. Enzymes are catalysts which influence chemical processes ensuring that necessary substances are made available to the mitochondria within the cells that supply the neurotransmitter. The significance of diet on effective neurotransmission will be discussed later in this chapter.

The development of the Central Nervous System (CNS)

The neurones form increasingly complex neural networks which are the basis of the nervous system. The nervous system is divided into two parts:

1. The brain stem and limbic system have evolved to understand the signals within the body. They respond to feelings such as hunger and anxiety and are connected to a variety of body organs, the endocrine system and the autonomous nervous system. These systems are responsible for regulating heart beat, respiration and digestion. They also determine the body's sleep cycle.

2. The thalamo-cortical system consists of the thalamus and the cortex acting together to receive signals external to the body. The cortex is adapted to receive signals from the sensors which respond to sight, touch, taste, smell, hearing and the body's awareness of its position in space.

Although it is only one quarter of the brain's total volume, the cortex contains 75 per cent of its 10 billion neurones. The function of these specialised neurones is to transfer signals from one part of the nervous system to another. The cortex is where much of the higher brain function is located.

The central nervous system begins to specialise at a very early stage: from the third week after conception a groove appears in the developing embryo which will form the basis of the spinal cord. After five weeks cells within the developing embryo specialise and form the nervous system. At eight weeks there is evidence of the first 'brain spurt' which results in the formation over a five week period of billions of cells called 'neuroblasts' – which develop into neurones. It is the total number of neuroblasts which determines the number of nerve cells and adequate nutrition for the infant at this critical stage is essential.

The most significant aspect of brain development occurs at 30 weeks gestation and continues for the first two years of life. This is the period when the nerve cells form most of their interconnections. The crucial factor in determining intellectual ability is not the number of neurones but the number of connections between them.

Studies have indicated that a maternal diet low in LCPs may delay foetal myelination and brain maturation leading to low birth weight and subsequent learning and behavioural disorders. The placenta concentrates LCPs by up to eight times and there is a correlation between brain circumference and the presence of arachidonic acid in the placental blood supply.

During the first months of life the brain requires large amounts of essential fatty acids to ensure appropriate development. In the mid-1980s research focused on the production of specially formulated milk products for babies who were premature or small for dates and could not be breast fed. This pre-term formula milk was higher in protein, carbohydrate and fat content than readily available formula milk. In 1990 Professor Alan Lucas reported on the results of a study in Glasgow which compared the development of pre-term and small for dates babies who were fed either the pre-term or ordinary formula milk. As expected those children fed with pre-term formula milk showed a significant IQ advantage when assessed at 18 months. One important feature of this study was to identify that children given the pre-term formula milk in periods in excess of a month, did not show any advantage over those fed for only that period.

In 1992 Lucas reported on a similar study where a comparison had been made between pre-term babies fed on their mother's own breast milk, donor breast milk or pre-term formula milk. The youngsters were assessed at the age of eight and it had been expected that those having access to pre-term formula milk would show the greatest advantage. This was not the case. The youngsters who had been given their mother's own breast milk were those who achieved the highest scores in indicators of intellectual ability. It was evident from this study that although there were some advantages with the improved nutritional content of pre-term formula milk, the mother's own breast milk offered the best start in life.

Further investigation showed that the significant factor was not a higher concentration of protein, fat and carbohydrate but another essential nutrient, docosahexanoic acid (DHA).

Research (Neuringer *et al.* 1988, Makrides *et al.* 1994, Farquharson *et al.* 1995) attempted to measure the DHA content in the cerebral cortex from birth to the age of two. The studies concluded that breast-fed infants did have greater levels of cerebral-cortex DHA than infants who were formula fed, suggesting that supply of DHA is dependent on diet.

In the fifth week of pregnancy (when cell division is most active and just before the first 'brain spurt'), and in the last trimester (the second 'brain spurt'), the DHA content in the cortex increases to between three and five times its normal level. The proportion of DHA was higher in breast-fed infants. Additional research (Crawford 1996) showed that in pre-term infants, blood levels of DHA were below that expected at term. Furthermore, two weeks after delivery the level of DHA had reduced to a third of that expected as compared with a control group of youngsters at the same stage of development. For pre-term babies it is crucial, therefore, to ensure that they have access to appropriate nutrients high in DHA. Concern over fat intake has led to a decline in the consumption of DHA and as a result the DHA content of breast milk has also reduced and this can have consequences for the developing infant. The impact of low DHA intake on neurological functioning in adults is also the subject of ongoing investigations. Results of studies published so far suggest that DHA levels have been measured and shown to be low in adults with a variety of psychiatric disorders and a high proportion of children with Attention Deficit and Hyperactivity Disorder.

The United Nations Food and Agriculture Organisation and the World Health Organisation Joint Expert Committee on Fats and Oils in Human Nutrition has recommended adding DHA to infant formula milks at levels historically found in breast milk.

The development of neural networks

The connections between nerve cells (neural networks) are affected by the messages the brain receives from the environment. Connections are continually being made and broken.

Esther Thelen, a developmental psychologist at the University of Indiana, completed a study of babies and produced evidence that the child begins to select behaviours which will become the building blocks for later development (Thelen 1989).

A month old baby is able to fixate on an object placed in its line of vision. At two months the baby is able to make anticipatory actions towards the object with a closed fist. However, at this stage the baby is still unable to co-ordinate its movements. In Dr Thelen's study she attached motion sensors to the limbs of babies which tracked and recorded such movements. After analysis, this provided valuable information as to how skills are acquired. Observation of a child aged six months indicated that movement was much more purposeful and directed in that the child could reach and grasp appropriately.

It had been believed that skills such as learning to reach were genetically programmed, however this research confirmed that the child solves for itself the sequence of instructions required to perform actions. The baby has a range of movements and chooses the ones which work. Initially the baby produces a series of random movements in all four limbs, making associated facial gestures. Occasionally, by chance, a movement achieves the desired outcome (the child touches the toy). Over time these actions are 'programmed' in the brain and become 'reflexive'. The child is then able to exert some control over its environment.

The neural pathways which produce purposeful behaviour are those which are reinforced and the idea that such connections are formed through a process of natural selection was proposed by Gerald Edelman in his book *Neural Darwinism. The Theory of Neuronal Group Selection* (1989). Furthermore, as the complexity of the connections increases the actual neural pathway becomes easier to trigger; since there are more synapses to transfer electrical pulses, the pulse will travel faster through the network.

In the simplified diagram below (Figure 2.3) the purpose of transmission is to transfer information from neurone A to neurone B. Applying an impulse at A causes a pulse through four other synapses to B (as well as to synapses G, C and D which

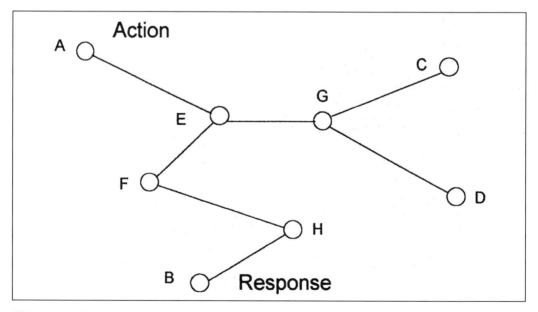

Figure 2.3 Developing neural network

causes either no reaction or an undesired reaction). This describes the action of a neurologically immature network. Owing to the lack of connections and the fact that several impulses are required to reach the necessary threshold for onward transmission, a pulse will take some time to travel from A to B and may be lost altogether. If, for example, five pulses are needed for transmission then:

H will need to receive five pulses before transmitting one pulse towards B
F will need to receive five pulses before transmitting one pulse towards H
E will need to receive five pulses before transmitting one pulse towards F
For every 125 pulses that E receives only one will reach B.

If we consider a more mature network (Figure 2.4) in this diagram extra linkages have been made (A-G), (A-F), (F-B), (G-H), (E-H) and the connections G-C and G-D have been 'pruned' as a consequence of not being beneficial.

In this mature network when A sends the same 125 pulses:
E receives 125 pulses and thus sends 25 to F, G and H
F receives 125 pulses from A, 25 from E (150) and sends 30 to B and H
G receives 125 pulses from A, 25 from E (150) and sends 30 to H
H receives 25 pulses from E, 30 from F, and 30 from G (85): sends 17 to B
B receives 47 pulses

Increasing the complexity of the network and creating shorter pathways through it can dramatically increase the speed of processing.

Connections do not have to form in a specific way (Edelman 1989). In the diagrams beneficial connection could have appeared between D and H or G and F still resulting in improved transmission of the pulse.

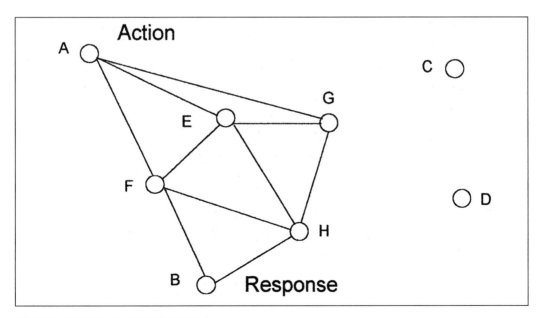

Figure 2.4 Mature neural network

It is apparent that there are two main factors affecting the speed at which pulses can travel through the brain:
- the complexity of the neural network
- the effectiveness of transmission of a pulse at the synapse between the nerve cells.

The brain reacts to the environment as it learns from experience. A stimulating environment encourages network formation and results in the improvement of the brain's ability to react, learn and memorise – its 'intelligence'.

As this process continues there are far more connections made than are necessary. Many of these pathways will have no useful purpose and by the age of three it is expected that a third will be 'pruned'. Pruning occurs simultaneously with the developmental process. Unnecessary connections 'die' while those which produce purposeful outcomes are reinforced (Figure 2.5).

This combination of the early development of neural networks and subsequent pruning means that a twelve month child has significantly more pathways than the adult. Where the brain has not successfully reinforced the appropriate neural pathways, messages are more likely to travel along extended routes, increasing the time required for processing. In addition there is a greater risk that the information will not reach the required destination. It is this persistent neurological immaturity which is the basis for the difficulties evident in youngsters with dyspraxia.

Efficient brain function depends on the successful transfer of information between the limbic and cortical systems. The cortex comprises a left and right hemisphere each with different properties which will be discussed in Chapter 3.

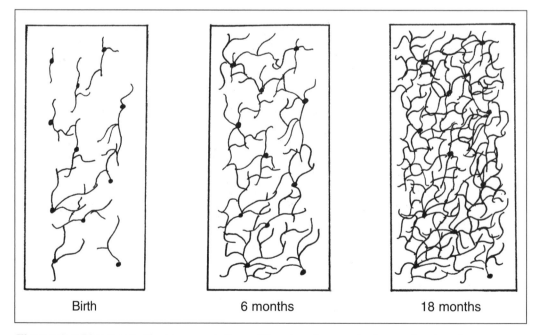

| Birth | 6 months | 18 months |

Figure 2.5 Diagrammatic representation of the development of neural networks

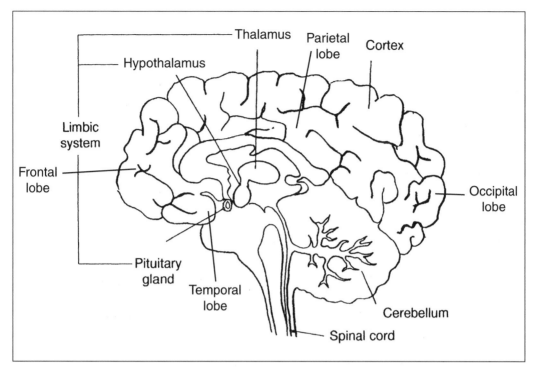

Figure 2.6 Position of the limbic system

In addition there are four cortical lobes (see Figure 2.6) with specific functions:
- the frontal lobes which are responsible for organisation, voluntary movement, planning purposeful activity and the production of speech;
- the parietal lobes which process the body's responses to touch, pain and temperature and co-ordinate joint and muscle positions;
- the occipital lobes which analyse messages from the retina before they are transformed to the parietal lobe for integration with additional perceptual information;
- the temporal lobes which interpret auditory stimuli. The left temporal lobe regulates the understanding and processing of language.

There are also some parts of the cortex which do not appear to have a specific function. These 'association' areas integrate the information 'received' from other parts of the brain.

The first chapter considered the comorbidity of developmental disorders. The characteristics of each have their origins in the dysfunctional transmission and interpretation of 'messages' within the systems of the brain. A great deal of research has focused on the identification of such 'origins' in an attempt to ensure that an accurate diagnosis of the disorder(s) is made.

Current opinion regarding autism and Asperger's Disorder identify biological and neurological origins. Shreibman (1988) reports evidence of unusually high levels of neurotransmitter materials particularly serotonin which is a neural opiate.

Courchesne (1991) identifies some cortical dysfunction. Shattock and Savery (1997) has studied the action of peptides and their effect on neurotransmission. These peptides which result from the incomplete breakdown of certain foods, in particular gluten from wheat and casein from milk, may have opioid action. The presence of this intense opioid activity would result in a disruption in the ability of the central nervous system to interpret information. Perception, cognitive ability, emotion mood and behaviour would all be impaired. The functions of the cerebral cortex would also be affected (Ozonoff *et al* 1994) and the many diverse symptoms of autism would result.

Specific learning difficulties such as dyspraxia and dyslexia occur when the cortex persists in a state of immaturity. There has been insufficient 'pruning' and information necessarily takes longer to process. Dyspraxia is the result of such immaturity in the right hemisphere, dyslexia the left.

Abnormalities attributed to early brain development are found in neuroanatomical studies of young adults with dyslexia. Underdeveloped temporal-parietal (auditory processing in syntax) and parieto-occipital (visual processing) regions in the left hemisphere have been identified. (Filipek 1995).

The behaviours and developmental profiles associated with dyspraxia are discussed in later chapters but reference should be made to research published in 1999. Since 1988 I have had the opportunity to assess more than 600 children and young adults. The majority displayed the expected 'symptoms' with a predictable developmental history. However, 18 per cent did not. In this group 70 per cent had significant feeding problems from birth and many mothers failed to gain weight appropriately during pregnancy. The origins of their difficulties were more likely to be metabolic – an inability to synthesise LCPs reducing the effectiveness of neural transmission.

There will be further discussion in relation to the neurological and metabolic basis of developmental disorders later.

Chapter 3

Developmental differences between the sexes

The cortex comprises two hemispheres, connected by a 'cable' of nerves, the corpus callosum. The left hemisphere receives sensory information from and controls the right side of the body while the right hemisphere controls the left.

The different functions of the two hemispheres have been identified through the assessment of electrical activity evident when the individual performs specific tasks.

The Left Hemisphere specialises in processing information sequentially. It is described as analytical because it interprets information piece by piece, recognising the parts which make up the whole. Although it is most efficient at processing verbal information, language should not be considered to be 'in' the left hemisphere. In addition, the left hemisphere can recognise that one stimulus comes before another. Verbal perception and the subsequent generation of language depends on awareness of the sequence in which sounds occur. To produce a written sentence, the idea is translated into smaller phrases and then words. The words are broken down into letters which must be reproduced on paper in the correct sequence. This represents a sequential analytical process.

The Right Hemisphere specialises in combining the parts which make a whole. Unlike the left hemisphere which processes information in a linear manner, the right hemisphere organises simultaneously. It uses a method of processing which perceives depth and constructs patterns. It is more efficient at visual and spatial processing (images). It also appears to be more sensitive to the melody and rhythmical aspects of music. Its language capacity (particularly in males) is limited and words play little part in its functioning. While both hemispheres process sensory information, it is thought that non-verbal stimuli are processed primarily in the right hemisphere. Facial recognition is an example of right-hemispheric function. The features are not analysed step by step, instead they are synthesised simultaneously: consequently information is processed more quickly in the right hemisphere. Figure 3.1 compares the differences in functioning between the left and right hemisphere.

The purpose of hemispheric specialisation is to improve the efficiency of the brain. Each hemisphere undertakes an analysis of information and transfers to the other hemisphere, if required, after a significant degree of processing has already occurred.

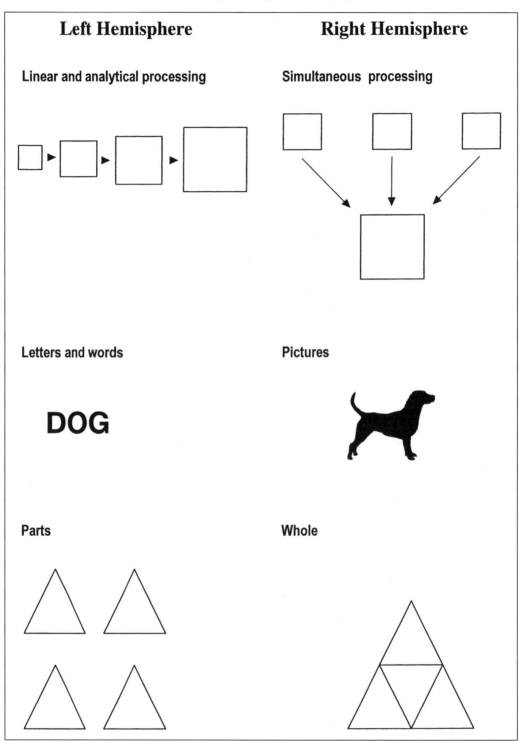

Figure 3.1 Diagrammatic representation of the processing differences between the left and right hemispheres

The notion of cerebral 'dominance' is a reflection of the development of the individual's neural circuits. Assessment of the learning styles and cognitive abilities of young children gives great insight into the development of function in the right and left hemispheres and consideration must be given to the differences between the sexes.

Developmental differences

Research into the specialisation of the right and left hemispheres shows that it is necessary to have effective processing in both sides of the brain for optimum efficiency. Encouraging the development of one hemisphere can result in an improved processing ability in the other.

Rauscher (1994) reported that preschool children given piano and singing lessons improved significantly in maths and complex spatial reasoning tasks, for example completing mazes, drawing geometric figures and copying patterns, compared with their controls. Differences in the brain function of males and females are programmed six weeks after conception. Production of the male hormone testosterone is triggered by the Y chromosome and consequently boys are exposed to five times more male hormones than girls. The female foetus is exposed to a small amount of testosterone from the mother's adrenal gland. It is hormones which are responsible for the characteristics of behaviour in boys and girls. Boys, on average, are better at solving three dimensional puzzles (right hemisphere) while girls are more verbally fluent (left hemisphere). Girls from birth are more interested in faces and sounds, boys are more interested in objects. The difference relates to the greater use of one hemisphere or the other. Evidence is emerging which suggests that it is the testosterone in the prenatal period which contributes to the subsequent spatial ability of the child.

Observation of developing skills during infancy provides evidence to support the theory that boys and girls learn at different rates. It also confirms that language skills develop more quickly in girls while boys spend more time improving spatial/perceptual skills. This remains in evidence until adulthood.

The potential for learning is present from the very early months of infancy: the nerve cells in the brain are in place. In the previous chapter research evidence was cited showing that it is the number of interconnections between the nerve cells which determines 'intelligence', not the number of nerve cells. It is important, therefore, that the child has access to an enriched environment to ensure appropriate development. Rosenzweig and his colleagues at the University of California (Berkeley) provided such an enriched environment to a group of young rats. They were allowed to grow in a cage which offered access to high levels of motor activity, ladders, wheels and tunnels, and they were provided with an adequate diet enriched with essential nutrients. The researchers had expected that there would be a change in enzyme levels but after 105 days, when the brains of the rats were examined, it was found that although the number of nerve cells had not increased in the group of 'enriched' rats, the fibres extending from the cells were more prolific and they were making more interconnections with other nerve cells.

The areas responsible for speech and language processing are typically located in the left hemisphere. However, the specialisation for this language processing follows a developmental progression. Studies by Talay-Senkal (1978) suggested that there was no hemispheric preference in visual and auditory language processing in youngsters up to the age of three. Subsequently a preference became more evident and was well established by the age of six. This progression continues to the age of twelve years when the process is virtually complete.

Research which shows that young children can recover speech and language after an injury to the left hemisphere is evidence of this development and it confirms that there is the opportunity to evolve other strategies to overcome 'damage'. As this organisation becomes irreversibly established by puberty, the extent of recovery from such injury diminishes. Account must also be taken of the significant differences in recovery of language ability in males and females beyond puberty where there has been an insult to the left hemisphere.

Recent research undertaken by Shaywitz at Yale University's Centre for Learning and Attention has assessed the activity in different parts of the brain through an imaging technique called functional MRI. This imaging technique was used to assess the area of the brain responsible for the processing of language. An experiment was set up and males were asked to look for rhyming words. The scan revealed that electrical activity was almost exclusively based in the left hemisphere. By comparison women activated centres in the left and right hemispheres. The purpose of the MRI scan was to make neural systems visible. The question was asked as to whether these differences in brain activity could explain the differences observed in the expressive language capabilities of men and women (Figure 3.2).

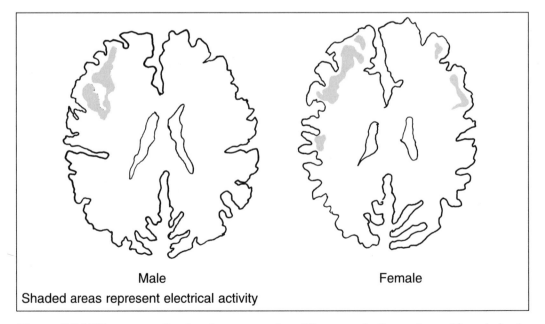

Male　　　　　　　　　　　　　　　　Female

Shaded areas represent electrical activity

Figure 3.2 MRI scan results showing processing differences in the male and female brain

A further experiment was undertaken to measure spatial ability. Here the subjects were asked to imagine an object in three dimensions, rotate it in the mind and select the matching shape. More than 75 per cent of males in the study scored above average.

At the University of Iowa EEGs were carried out to record electrical activity in the cortex in tasks which would be predominantly based in the right hemisphere. The subject was asked to match the circle with the correct arc (Figure 3.3).

The test required good mental imagery. The right hemisphere of the brain has a neural network which is designed to process visual stimulation. The test also measured spatial ability. Again the evidence suggested that boys used the right hemisphere and girls used both. The girls are therefore using additional cortical resources which is evident in that both sides of the brain are being used. As females have brains which are more highly developed in language skills and skewed towards verbal processing there is a negative side. It is possible that this leaves less room for spatial processing but it also suggests that girls employ visual and verbal strategies which are less effective when solving three dimensional problems.

Females have the capacity to analyse information using both hemispheres simultaneously. Males appear to have evolved specialised functions whereby the left hemisphere processes language and the right spatial/visual stimuli. This has a significant impact on learning difficulties. If a female has a processing difficulty in the left hemisphere there are other 'systems' which can be utilised in the right. In males this is not the case and this difference could explain why significantly more males than females (4:1) are identified with dyslexia.

Figure 3.3 Patterns observed during testing

Similarly, where there are difficulties in processing information in the right hemisphere (dyspraxia) the male is unable to access the function in the left hemisphere. The ratio of males to females identified with dyspraxia is also 4:1.

Females may be less effective with perceptual processing. The male focuses all his resources and utilises the capacity of the right frontal lobe to generate an image: the female relies on verbally based strategies. The obvious disadvantage is that for males this is an 'all or nothing' response: there are few 'backup systems' if those in the right hemisphere break down.

Stages of development

During the first 12 months there is evidence of great improvement in motor skills, language and perception. The child would be expected to have achieved independent sitting, to have rolled from side to side and pulled itself to a standing position. Crawling would have been an integral part of this process and the child would become independently mobile usually by the age of 14 months.

First words appear and the child is able to say 'mama' and 'dada'. Short babbled sentences of six or more syllables occur but generally there is a marked difference between the abilities of boys and girls at 12 months. Both boys and girls show that they have inquisitive minds and they respond to brightly coloured objects presented in a variety of shapes.

Gross and fine motor skills continue to develop during the next 12 months, and girls continue to extend their vocabulary. Boys, meanwhile, prefer to engage in more practical activities, extending play with shapes and enjoying jigsaws, shape sorters and traditional equipment such as Megablocks and Lego.

By the time the children are due to enter the nursery environment between the ages of three and four there are marked differences between the abilities of boys and girls. The boys, given 'free choice', will usually opt for the more practical, outdoor activities where they have the opportunity to change frequently from one area to another. In contrast, even as young as three, girls are more likely to spend time looking at books and using pencils, crayons and paint to show their creativity.

As well as marked sex differences in the development of language and perceptual skills there are also differences in social behaviours. The social environment has a major effect on development but there is overwhelming evidence to suggest that it interacts with inherent predispositions. Although we are profoundly influenced by social forces around us, the competitive and aggressive behaviour has its origin in the biological nature of boys. Male and female brains are 'wired' differently as we know: in general terms, language is processed in both the right and left hemispheres by girls but only in the left hemisphere by boys.

Between the ages of four and seven boys present as being more active, with significantly limited concentration when compared with girls. The boys continue to choose outdoor activities and toys which are mechanical. Their play involves much more physical contact with other children which sometimes translates into aggressive challenging.

Children from the age of four generally choose to play in single sex groups. Girls settle down and concentrate; boys interrupt what they are doing five times more frequently than girls. Girls on average spend twice as long on any task.

Boys play fight and engage in rough and tumble, they are much more challenging than girls and in the main there is an element of competitiveness in their play. They build towers to see how high they are and they will try to compete with other youngsters to build higher than anyone else. Girls, on the other hand, are much more cooperative: they take turns and attempt to include group members. The well-developed verbal ability of females continues throughout life into adulthood. On average women do better on verbal tests, as demonstrated when a group of teenagers were given a word and asked to write down other words with the same meaning. Five times as many girls scored at the top end of the scale – boys in contrast had a much higher incidence of spelling and grammatical errors.

Until the age of four girls and boys function predominantly in the right hemisphere. Evidence suggests that girls then begin to show increasing levels of activity in the left hemisphere and to process information sequentially. They are now at the most appropriate stage in development to access a structured programme for reading – letter recognition, word building, sequencing and sentence formation.

If the child is then presented with a formalised educational setting where such programmes of learning are available the female is more easily able to adapt. The children are introduced to letters which are then compared with corresponding sounds. The letters make words and the words make sentences. This progression is easy to understand if the left hemisphere is at the right stage of processing. Unfortunately, for boys, in many cases, this is not yet the achieved stage of development. Boys are continuing to develop their perceptual skills and persist in spending much less time on task than girls: concentration rarely exceeds five minutes.

Often the transition between right and left hemispheric functioning does not take place until approximately the age of six in boys. By this time they may have already become disaffected with the education system: they have not moved beyond the first level of the reading scheme. Where there is evidence of neurological immaturity this transfer can take place at a much later stage. Boys again are disadvantaged: if they have not developed the appropriate method for analysing letters and words until the age of eight they will be well behind the rest of their peer group. It is hardly surprising that on entry to Key Stage 2 there are five times more boys than girls with significant reading problems. Perhaps if they were given access to an accelerated learning programme at the age of seven or eight many of the differences between the sexes would diminish.

In summary: the research evidence cited in this chapter compares the differences in hemispheric functioning between the brains of males and females. Female brains use both hemispheres to process language (predominantly a left hemispheric function) and spatial tasks (predominantly a right hemispheric function). Where there is evidence of immaturity in the left hemisphere the characteristic presenting symptoms are those of dyslexia. Where the immaturity is based in the right hemisphere then the symptoms are those of dyspraxia. Statistics inform us that the ratio of boys to girls with both conditions is somewhere in the region of 4 or 5 to 1. The incidence of girls identified as having either difficulty will be reduced because of the residual functioning in the opposing hemisphere.

If there are difficulties with the left hemisphere in boys they do not have any additional backup systems and so the problem persists. In females, where both sides of the brain have operative function, the difficulties will be reduced, in many cases to a level where they are not significant. If we can offer an educational environment which addresses the learning style of males and females then the outcomes for both sets of pupils will be improved. To encourage boys to achieve at a higher level there has to be a requirement to offer a more visual approach: the use of diagrams is invaluable. Equality of education does not mean that males and females have to do the same thing: boys and girls learn in different ways so to give boys an equal chance, biological differences should be taken into account.

Chapter 4

Observable characteristics

The focus of this chapter is to determine whether there are identifiable characteristics evident at key stages during the child's development which would lead to a subsequent diagnosis of developmental dyspraxia. This information is based on my personal assessment of more than 400 children and young adults aged between 2 and 28, interviews with their parents wherever possible and access to additional information from general practitioners, paediatricians, child and adolescent psychiatrists, health visitors, clinical psychologists, speech therapists, occupational and physiotherapists and optometrists. The proformas used to compile this information are provided in Chapter 6.

Developmental dyspraxia is the term used to describe youngsters and adults who have co-ordination difficulties but who also, in the majority of cases, show significant perceptual problems. Confusion can arise when the word 'dyspraxia' is taken in its literal sense, i.e. meaning unco-ordinated, and used to describe the symptoms of known neurological conditions such as cerebral palsy, hemiplegia or muscular dystrophy.

The Dyspraxia Foundation describes dyspraxia as follows: 'It is an impairment or immaturity in the organisation of movement. Associated with this there may be problems of language, perception and thought.'

Developmental dyspraxia affects between two and five per cent of the population with a ratio of four boys to every girl. It can have a devastating affect on the performance of youngsters if their difficulties are not acknowledged while still at school. Early identification can ameliorate many of these problems and ensure that the child does not suffer through the loss of self-esteem which is evident in many cases.

In Chapter 2 consideration was given to the neurological basis of dyspraxia and the significance of diet. Where there is evidence that the origin of the condition is likely to be metabolic, factors are apparent before birth. They include:

- Small for dates
- Prematurity
- Poor maternal diet
- Failure to gain weight appropriately during pregnancy
- Sickness throughout pregnancy

- Family history of food allergy or intolerance (dairy produce, wheat)
- Family history of eczema/asthma
- Family history of coeliac disease.

From birth the majority of the youngsters, irrespective of the basis for their difficulties (neurological/metabolic), follow a specific pattern of development. The characteristics identified in more than 70 per cent of the sample population assessed are shown in Figure 4.1.

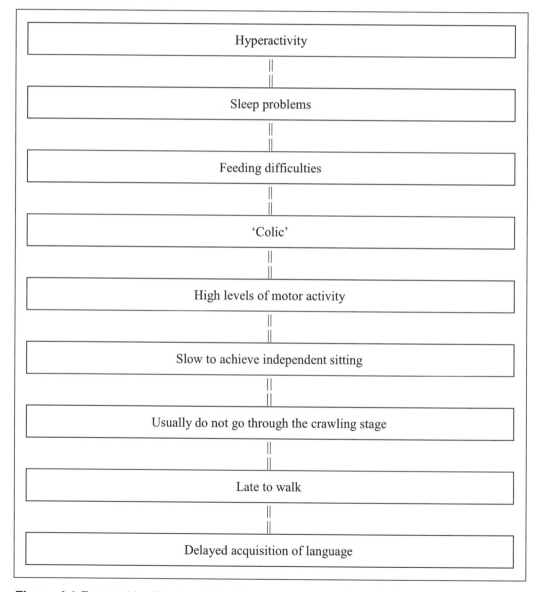

Figure 4.1 Factors identified in 70% of the sample population studied

Gubbay (1985) suggested that in perhaps 50 per cent of diagnosed cases of dyspraxia significant factors are evident during pregnancy, labour and birth. Interviews with parents of youngsters in my sample population highlighted difficulties in 82 per cent of the cases. They included:

- Prolonged labour
- Prematurity (birth before 38 weeks)
- Postmaturity (birth after 42 weeks).

The children presented as hyperactive from birth. They responded inappropriately to external stimulation. They were disturbed by changes in light intensity, noise and strong smells. They were youngsters who required high levels of adult involvement and constant reassurance. A parent said:

> He was just different from my other children. He always appeared more vulnerable and from birth I just felt he needed more of my time, more protection. For the first six months he was virtually strapped to me continuously: while I washed, shopped and attended fitness classes at the gym. He cried continuously whenever I left him. At the age of four he still followed me around the house, even when I went to the bathroom.

Sleep problems persisted often until the age of seven or eight when children would complain of night terrors. It was very difficult to develop any sort of sleeping routine with the children settling often for periods of up to an hour but then awake and distressed for the rest of the time. In one case, the parents took it in turns to walk the floor all night with the child semi-upright in his pushchair. When placed in his cot he would bring his knees to his chest as though in pain and cry constantly. The pushchair routine continued throughout the first year.

Feeding difficulties may also be identified before birth. More than 60 per cent of the babies were small for dates or born prematurely. A great many of these children were unable to breast-feed successfully and were placed on formula milk products. Some transferred to soya milk when they failed to gain weight or showed an adverse reaction to cows, milk: 12 per cent of my sample were labelled as 'failing to thrive' under 12 months.

Colic was evident in many of the children and this persisted beyond the expected time scales. Parents reported that their children were not just mildly distressed but were in continuing discomfort until their knees were supported close to their chest.

High levels of motor activity were reported: the children continued to make reaching and grasping movements with limited success. There is evidence to suggest that the development of the expected neural pathways is reduced.

In more than 50 per cent of the cases studied the youngsters were not sitting independently until eight months or more and many were unable to roll appropriately from supine to prone positions at the expected stage of development.

More than 80 per cent of the sample population did not go through the crawling stage. Many 'bottom shuffled' and pulled to standing at approximately 14 to 16 months, walking independently at 18 months. Some children who did not go through the crawling stage pulled to standing much earlier and walked independently at 12 months. There seems to be almost an inbuilt mechanism whereby these youngsters overcame the problems of co-ordinating four limbs independently by overriding this developmental stage and moved towards co-ordinating just two limbs – the legs.

The youngsters were often late to develop independent walking skills and continued to trip or bump into things in the nursery and early years environments.

The acquisition of language skills must be assessed accurately. For youngsters with developmental dyspraxia 50 per cent show evidence of late acquisition of a single word vocabulary with significant articulation problems until the age of eight or nine. Although speech and language skills are delayed they still follow the expected developmental progression albeit more slowly. The presenting problems are usually the result of an inability to co-ordinate the speech apparatus. This will be discussed further in Chapter 6. Where there was evidence of disordered language or poor comprehension skills it was symptomatic of other disorders which may well be occurring comorbidly with dyspraxia.

Many parents have difficulty persuading professionals that their child is experiencing problems. While it is accepted that children do develop at different rates, where a number of features of a developmental disorder are present nothing is lost through early intervention and a great deal can be gained. Often it is only when the child is placed with a preschool provider i.e. playgroup or nursery that poor co-ordination and perceptual problems are acknowledged.

Assessment of youngsters at an early stage can be difficult if we are seeking a 'label'. In young children the comorbidity of developmental disorders is possibly as high as 60 per cent and structured low-level intervention in the early years has been shown to have a dramatic effect on the development of skills (Wetton 1997). Early identification is beneficial not only to the child but also the family. This is discussed further in Chapter 7 with recommended programmes of intervention in Chapter 8.

Observable behaviours up to the age of three

- Persistent feeding difficulties
  - food intolerance
  - child will accept only a restricted diet (preference given to food which is pureed).
- Evidence of sleeping difficulties
  - child does not follow expected bedtime routines, constantly waking during the night and requiring reassurance.
- Uncoordinated movement
  - unsteady when walking independently, falls easily and may move with a wide gait
  - unable to move one foot without overbalancing
  - unable to pedal a tricycle and prefers using sit-astride toys which do not require hands and feet to be co-ordinated simultaneously.

- Difficulties with fine motor skills
  - has problems manipulating pegs and takes longer than expected to complete the task
  - avoids scribbling and using crayons and pencils because of difficulty in holding the implement.
- High levels of motor activity
  - constantly on the go
  - may have continuous arm movements even when sitting.
- Sensitive to high levels of noise or changes in light intensity.
- Toilet training (particularly bowel control) may be delayed.
- Avoidance of constructional toys
  - shows little interest in Lego, jigsaws and inset puzzles and finds tower building very difficult.
- Delayed language development
  - can make initial sounds 'mm' but has difficulty articulating single words.
- Difficulties with articulation rather than comprehension.
- Highly emotional
  - easily distressed with frequent outbursts of uncontrolled behaviour.
- Concentration very limited
  - child usually able to remain for only two to three minutes on any task.

Dyspraxic children in the nursery are already identified as being different from the rest. They are excluded from cooperative games enjoyed by other youngsters because their behaviour is too erratic and they are often unable to understand the 'rules'. Psychological barriers to progress can be in place before formal schooling begins.

Observable behaviour in the nursery

- Insecurity
  - problems separating from adult.
- High levels of motor activity
  - unable to remain seated or stay in one place for periods in excess of five minutes
  - when concentrating on an activity feet swing and tap persistently
  - hands clapping together or twisting when excited.
- High levels of excitability
  - voice is often loud and shrill
  - very demanding with evidence of temper tantrums for no apparent reason
  - becomes very easily distressed particularly when arrangements are not adhered to: if the child is expecting to follow a particular activity and the plan is altered.

- Problems with co-ordination
  - walks on tiptoes with poor balance and hands waving
  - dislikes climbing activities; children can be anxious with heights
  - constantly bumping into objects and falling over
  - evidence of associated movements in the hands when feet are moving, hands flap when the child is running or jumping. (discussed in Chapter 5)
- Difficulties pedalling
  - problems continue with the co-ordination of foot and hand movements. The child is unable to 'steer' the toy while pedalling.
- Poor figure ground awareness
  - no sense of danger, jumps from inappropriate heights
  - misinterpretation of information, a crack in the pavement or the edge of a tile in the floor can be perceived as an obstacle which must be climbed.
- Feeding difficulties persist
  - often follows a restricted diet
  - eating can be problematic since the children are unable to co-ordinate a knife and fork and often spill liquid from drinking cups. As a consequence they prefer to use fingers to feed.
- Avoids constructional toys
  - jigsaws, formboards, Lego and Megablocks are not enjoyable activities
  - these youngsters also have difficulty building blocks beyond two or three cubes.
- Poor fine motor skills
  - pencil grip immature, difficulty using scissors
  - drawings are very immature and often unrecognisable.
- Lack of imaginative play
  - the children can retell stories they have heard or videos they have watched but they find it difficult to engage in a different scenario even when the characters are the same.
- Perceived as very immature in comparison with peers.
- Peer group isolation
  - children are identified as being different: they have difficulties with cooperative play, they may also have communication difficulties and consequently play alongside rather than along with other children
  - prefer adult company.
- Laterality not established
  - problems crossing the midline
  - engaging activities on the right side of the body with the right hand, activities on the left side with the left hand.
- Evidence of delayed acquisition of language skills
  - children often referred to the speech therapist who is then the source of referral on to external agencies.

- Sensitive to sensory stimulation
  - dislikes high levels of noise
  - dislikes being touched
  - dislikes wearing new clothes particularly if the label is close to the skin
  - can be affected by changes in washing powder: clothes smell differently.
- Limited response to verbal instructions
  - response time is slow by comparison with peers
  - problems with auditory sequencing.
- Limited concentration
  - tasks often left unfinished, sometimes because they are perceived as too difficult
  - the children are often confused as to what they should be doing next and consequently are likely to engage in frequent changes in activity. (More evident in boys at this stage.)

Jamie: a case study

Jamie was the second of three children and born after a relatively unremarkable pregnancy. Mum reported that Jamie's progress had been closely monitored because she had had a miscarriage at four months, six months before the conception of Jamie. Jamie was born at 38 weeks weighing 7 lb. 0 oz after a labour lasting 11 hours.

He presented as irritable from birth and cried constantly. He was difficult to breast-feed and his weight dropped to under 7 lb. within a week of birth. He transferred to formula milk and could take small amounts on a one to two hourly basis. Mum reported that he only stopped crying when he was carried and rocked. Parents remembered spending many evenings travelling in the car to settle him during the first six months.

Although Jamie's older sister Rachel had achieved the expected developmental milestones comparisons were not made between the two because parents were told 'boys are generally behind girls in their early development'. He was nearly 12 months old when his first tooth appeared.

Despite high levels of irritability Jamie presented as an alert child who enjoyed 'listening' to adult conversations and looking at pictures. He detested activities such as stacking blocks and shape sorters. He hated the texture of furry toys and preferred a linen doll belonging to Rachel.

Feeding continued to be problematic and after a brief attempt with soya milk he returned to the original formula. At six months his parents encouraged Jamie to eat more textured food, which was virtually impossible. He choked, spat and cried at every attempt. Until the age of two and a half Jamie's mother prepared all his food using a liquidiser.

Jamie was sitting independently at nine and a half months and then bottom shuffled until he finally pulled to standing at 18 months. He took his first independent step at 20/21 months and he was walking, albeit unsteadily, at two years.

Jamie was offered two morning sessions at a local playgroup and he attended for three weeks. He responded very badly to the high levels of noise and he couldn't cope with children racing past him at speed on sit-astride toys or pushing mini shopping trolleys towards him.

At home he appeared to become more dependent on his mother and she was unable to leave the room without taking him with her. Anxieties rose further when he was offered a half-time place at a local nursery. He had not been fully toilet trained.

Until 14/16 months his bowels had never been able to produce 'proper' stools. They seemed to move between extremes, mostly very hard and compacted but sometimes very loose. This had been attributed to 'poor' diet and he had been given large doses of Lactulose. Jamie's mother believed that he 'just didn't seem to get the right messages to open his bowels'.

Initially the problem was avoided because Jamie refused to use the toilet in nursery. As time passed he became very anxious about it and until the age of six refused to use any toilet other than the one at home.

In the nursery environment Jamie presented as a loner. He was quickly identified by the other pupils as being different from them and he was not included in their imaginative games. His co-ordination was poor and he was constantly bumping into objects and other children. He was a child who was never invited home to anyone else's house for tea.

The nursery staff themselves were concerned about a number of factors:

- His isolation within the peer group and apparently limited social skills.
- His development of self-help skills, e.g. toilet training and dressing, appeared to be behind the rest of his peer group.
- He would play happily in the water and sand but resisted the construction table and the 'writing' table and he refused to undertake any imaginative play.

Some of his behaviour had been described as 'repetitive' as he could repeat at length stories from videos such as 'Fireman Sam' and Disney films watched in the home environment.

If Jamie's assessment had been based solely on the observation of his behaviour he might have been diagnosed as a youngster with a communication disorder. However, developmental history, motor assessment and psychometric profile confirmed that he was a youngster displaying many of the symptoms of developmental dyspraxia.

Additional assessment information (chronological age four years nine months)

Jamie's articulation was poor but the content of his speech was age appropriate. Sucking had been a problem from birth and even at the age of four he was still unable to drink through a straw or blow bubbles. He could not co-ordinate his tongue, lips and soft palate in order to produce all of the expected speech sounds.

He was unable to pedal a tricycle and co-ordinate the movement of the handle bars at the same time to prevent crashing into objects. When observed on the climbing frame he did not put one foot in front of another but brought each foot independently to meet the next. He was terrified of any height more than 15 centimetres from the ground and became extremely anxious when asked to jump from a low step. While unable to crawl appropriately he could extend both hands and drag his knees to meet them. He could balance for two seconds on his right foot although his arms swung wildly. He could not balance on his left foot. He was unable to jump with two feet together and he could not hop. In addition, he was unable to walk heel to toe between two parallel lines 15 centimetres apart and he could not walk on his tiptoes.

He was anxious that samples of his drawings might be placed on the walls of the nursery – they were virtually scribbled pictures, often in dark colours. He could hold the crayons and pencils appropriately but was unable to copy simple shapes like a square, circle and cross. In addition, he had great difficulty completing a simple inset puzzle which would have been appropriate for a two year old.

Jamie's concentration varied dramatically. He could spend a great deal of time in the sand and water but found it difficult to concentrate for more than five or ten minutes at any other activity. He would move to outdoor play but did not participate easily in any of the activities. He was happy to sit in the trailer when another child pedalled the bicycle.

The nursery had used a developmental checklist to identify strengths and weaknesses. Cognitive ability in this type of assessment is dependent upon having good perceptual skills, e.g. Can the child complete an 'inset' puzzle or reproduce a pattern using coloured blocks? The resulting checklist suggested that Jamie had a generalised rather than a specific learning difficulty.

Assessment using the Wechsler Preschool and Primary Scale of Intelligence (WPPSI) highlighted a range of strengths and weaknesses in Jamie's cognitive profile and identified many skills in the average to above-average range. (Appropriate assessment tools are examined in Chapter 5.)

The 'repetitive' language was the result of practising the 'script' from the video in an attempt to make his speech comprehensible.

Outcome

Jamie had access to intervention programmes to develop his perceptual, motor, communication and social skills. He was never removed from his peer group and the structured activities always involved working with other pupils and sometimes the whole class.

At the end of Key Stage 1, Jamie had moved from Stage 3 to Stage 1 on the Special Needs Register.

When the child enters full-time schooling, the structure of the educational environment and the requirement that youngsters perform directed tasks highlights further difficulty.

Observable behaviours in the child of primary school age

- Organisational difficulties
  - difficulty adapting to a structured school routine
  - forgetting PE equipment or materials the class teacher has suggested are supplied from home
  - difficulty relaying messages from school to home.
- Continuing difficulties evident in PE
  - unco-ordinated movements
  - anxiety with heights
  - difficulty judging distances, for example, with ball throwing.
- Slow at dressing
  - buttons fastened in the wrong holes
  - clothes inadvertently placed back to front or inside out
  - unable to tie shoe laces (shoes with Velcro fasteners are recommended).
- Development of reading skills may be unaffected and progress follows a normal curve (50 per cent below and 50 per cent above average).
- Spelling is significantly affected and this is the result of a combination of difficulties with auditory sequencing and visual perception.
- Handwriting difficulties
  - excessive time required for completion of task
  - repetition and practice has little effect on the development of skills
  - copying skills are poor
  - drawings continue to be immature.
- Literal use of language
  (A parent reported that she had taken her son, aged nine, to a restaurant. The furnishings dated back to the mid 1800s and at one end of the room there was a large, imposing 'throne like' chair. The mother pointed towards it and said, 'I bet there is a story behind that'. Immediately her son ran over to investigate and said, 'I can't find any book behind here'.)
- Difficulty remembering instructions.
- Problems with auditory sequencing: skills can be improved by supplementing them with visual clues.
- Problems with concentration
  - difficulty remaining on task
  - high levels of motor activity interfere with written work and with class discussion
  - motor movements, e.g. foot tapping or hand flapping when concentrating or excited.
- Highly emotional
  - can become very involved in a sad fictional story and exhibit inappropriately high levels of distress
  - losing a pencil or not having the right book creates an overreaction.

- Problems with social relationships
  - problems with peer relationships often evident in the nursery environment persist throughout school
  - isolated within the classroom and in the playground
  - enjoys the security of relationships with adults
  - where 'friendships' are in evidence they are usually with much younger children.
- Physical symptoms
  - migraines, headaches and feeling sick.

Observable behaviours in pupils of secondary school age

- Difficulties with social relationships
  - child presents as a loner who states that he/she prefers his/her own company
  - through lack of experience does not engage in cooperative working with peer group. This can be difficult in the classroom environment where it is necessary to work with a partner, either in PE or for some curricular investigation.
- Difficulties in organisation
  - unable to follow a timetable
  - unable to produce the correct equipment
  - poor understanding of time and often arrives late for lessons or fails to arrange meetings with peers.
- Highly emotional
  - almost appears to have a personality disorder, exhibiting high levels of excitement at times and almost clinical depression at others
  - some youngsters may have developed phobias and/or obsessional or repetitive behaviour.
- Difficulties with co-ordination persist but they are often masked on entry to secondary education
  - can appear to be untidy with clothing inappropriately fastened
  - difficulty carrying equipment or school bags.
- Recording information
  - major difficulties experienced with work which must be committed to paper, handwriting is usually printed rather than cursive.
  - difficulties in the speed of information processing and instructions are not followed appropriately.
- Poor short-term visual and auditory memory
  - copying from the board
  - taking dictated notes.
- Easily led
  - continuing problems with the literal use of language and the youngsters believe everything that they are told
  - in a desperate attempt to gain friendship they will follow the direction of others in the peer group.

- Obsessional behaviours
  - evidence of some behaviours which have not previously been observed: the need to follow rigorous routines for setting out work, the development of nervous 'tics'.

Characteristics of adults with dyspraxia

- Attentional problems, poor concentration
  - when in conversation the discussion may often move off at a tangent and often it is difficult for them to provide direct answers to questions
  - concentration is poor and many adults display the symptoms of attention deficit and hyperactivity disorder.
- Language
  - speech can be loud and quickly produced. There can be additional problems with intonation and misinterpretation of the language they are hearing.
- Obsessional characteristics
  - many adults are identified as having obsessional compulsive disorder which is the result of developing routines to give their lives structure; some early signs may be evident during secondary schooling
  - obsessional behaviours are also evident because of continuing high levels of anxiety.
- Co-ordination difficulties
  - problems differentiating between left and right. This makes driving very difficult. In addition, there is the requirement to co-ordinate hands and feet simultaneously
  - adults identify themselves as 'a danger to be around', particularly lethal with tools and mechanical equipment.
- Poor handwriting
  - in adulthood this is usually overcome with access to word-processing facilities.
- Very low self-esteem.
- Very emotional
  - distressed when anything, however insignificant, goes wrong
  - very excited, unable to control emotions when, for example, watching adventure films (one adult said that he found it impossible to watch a tennis match – the tension wondering whether the ball would cross the net was unbearable).
- Unrealistic expectations
  - set impossible targets as if to prove they are incapable of high achievement.
- Inability to remember verbal instructions
  - overcome problems by compiling lists.
- Constant lateness for appointments
  - no concept of time.
- Inability to complete tasks quickly
  - information processing difficulties
  - problems in recording information.

- Decisions constantly altered
  - heavily influenced by the person they have last spoken to.
- Depression
  - often have clinical diagnosis made
  - linked with Obsessional-Compulsive Disorder.
- Difficulty maintaining relationships with peers
  - usually the result of having few friends in childhood so the 'testing' and development of social skills is not completed.
- Sleeping difficulties
  - adults report that they are unable to 'switch off'. The brain is being given constant reminders of tasks unfinished and events in the future which are causing anxiety.
- High comorbidity with ADHD and psychiatric illness.

Further information for parents and teachers working with children and adults with dyspraxia is presented in Chapter 10.

Chapter 5

Neuropsychological assessment

Discussion in the first two chapters focused on the similarities evident in the presenting symptoms of a number of developmental disorders: namely ADHD, dyspraxia, dyslexia and autistic spectrum disorder. To make an accurate 'diagnosis' of these conditions, given that comorbidity in young children is possibly as high as 60 per cent and in older pupils and young adults 45 per cent, assessment should include information about the individual's developmental history and a standardised test of cognitive functioning. The full range of information comes from a variety of sources:
- Parental observation
  - they are the first observers to evaluate the development of their child's motor skills and language acquisition.
- Formal observation
  - watching a child copy designs, pronounce words or solve problems in mathematics.
- Standardised assessment
  - Wechsler Intelligence Scales
  - Luria-Nebraska Neuropsychological Battery
  - Kaufman Assessment Battery for Children.

It is the Wechsler Intelligence Scales which are the most widely used measures to assess the cognitive ability of children (Reschly 1997) and they form the basis of my research to identify performance indicators within the battery of sub-tests which would provide a 'profile' of developmental dyspraxia. This will be discussed later in the chapter.

There has been a great deal of research already published about the psychometric properties of the Wechsler Scales and the interpretation of test scores. It is appropriate to offer some evidence as to its 'reliability' in the identification of other developmental disorders.

The Wechsler assessment provides a reference point for higher level cortical functions: it estimates intellectual potential or psychometric ability. A range of cognitive functions are evaluated so that the specific areas of difficulty can be targeted for intervention.

Neuropsychological assessment involves much more than testing and providing a series of individual sub-test scores. It is the interpretation of these scores seen in context with the individual's developmental history which provides evidence for 'diagnosis'. It is the experience the clinician brings to the assessment which makes it valid; psychological tests are not in themselves conclusive diagnostic indicators of specific disorders.

The Wechsler Intelligence Scales

They are:
- Wechsler Preschool and Primary Scale of Intelligence (WPPSI) (Age range 2–7 years).
- Wechsler Intelligence Scale for Children (WISC) (Age range 6–16.11)
- Wechsler Adult Intelligence Scale (WAIS) (Age range 17+)

They have undergone a number of revisions and depending on the date of the test are referred to as: (R) (Revised), III (3rd revision), III UK (3rd revision UK).

The WISC III UK comprises 13 sub-tests which are divided into assessments of verbal and non-verbal ability (Figure 5.1).

Verbal scores	Performance scores
Information	Picture completion
Similarities	Coding
Arithmetic	Picture arrangement
Vocabulary	Block design
Comprehension	Object assembly
(Digit span)	(Symbol search)
	(Mazes)

Figure 5.1 Summary of sub-tests of the WISC III UK

The sub-tests identified in brackets are supplementary, but provide important additional information if they are completed.

Format and purpose of each sub-test

Information
The child is asked to respond verbally to a series of questions which assess his general knowledge. They reflect how well information about the environment is absorbed. As the child progresses through primary and on into secondary education, he is expected to absorb more factual data from books. The pupil with reading difficulties may have problems with this test.

Similarities
The child is presented with two words such as 'chair' and 'table' and asked to say why they are the same. This reflects the child's understanding of language. The child is encouraged to give as much detail as possible in his response.

Arithmetic

This test relates to the child's general intellectual ability and he is required to respond orally to questions of mental arithmetic. Some youngsters perform much better giving verbal responses than when required to write down the answer.

Vocabulary

The child is asked to give the definitions of a series of single words and is encouraged to give as much information as possible. He often inserts the word into a sentence to convey the meaning.

Comprehension

The child is presented with a series of questions beginning: 'What should you do if...?' The responses give an indication of the child's social code. This assessment differs from reading comprehension tests where the child is asked questions which relate to the passage in which the answer can be found.

Digit span

The child is asked to repeat a series of numbers of increasing length forwards and backwards. The scaled score is based on the combined raw scores for digits forwards and digits backwards which may involve different cognitive processes, especially in certain clinical groups. For example: a study by Rudel and Denckla (1974) found that children with developmental disorders involving right-hemisphere deficits had impaired performance. The performance of dyspraxic youngsters highlights significant weaknesses in repeating the digits backwards. This assessment measures short-term ability to retain auditory sequential information. This test requires concentration and can present difficulties for children with attention deficits.

Picture completion

A series of coloured pictures is presented to the child and he is asked to identify which part is missing. This sub-test assesses the child's ability to concentrate and analyse data presented visually.

Coding

Younger children are required to draw a symbol inside a series of simple shapes. Older children (eight plus) copy symbols under a series of numbers. Youngsters with a poor short-term visual memory or significant visual motor problems experience particular difficulty with this sub-test because they are required to concentrate and co-ordinate eye and hand movements at speed.

Picture arrangement

A set of cards, each a picture, is mixed up and presented to the child. He is required to rearrange them into the sequence which correctly relates the story. This assesses the child's visual sequencing ability.

Block design

The child is given initially four cubes and then, as the designs become more complicated, nine cubes. A two-dimensional pattern is placed in front of the child who is then required to reproduce it using the cubes. This assesses the child's visual perceptual skills.

Object assembly

A set of jigsaw pieces is presented to the child who is required to assemble them in a recognisable form. The tasks become increasingly complex. This measures the child's ability to organise visually presented material into a whole from its component parts.

Symbol search

A series of paired groups of symbols is positioned on the left side of the page. The child scans the row to determine whether the symbols are present farther along. This requires concentration and the ability to co-ordinate eye movement to scan the page at speed.

Mazes

The child is given a starting point and using a pencil works his way through without crossing any of the lines. Good hand–eye co-ordination is needed.

In the Wechsler Preschool and Primary Scales the Coding and Picture arrangement sub-tests are replaced by Geometric design and Mazes. In the Wechsler Adult Scale Coding is replaced by Digit Symbol.

The scaled scores range from 1 to 19 (9–11 depicting the average). The verbal scores provide a verbal IQ (VIQ) and the performance scores a performance IQ (PIQ).

Research published relating performance on the WISC as being specific to locating brain dysfunction suggests that there is some correlative evidence to support the notion that verbal IQ reflects left-hemispheric functioning whereas the performance IQ reflects right-hemispheric functioning (Fedio and Mirsky 1969; Rourke *et al.* 1971, 1973). Similar types of conclusions with implications for clinical diagnosis have been offered for the verbal IQ/performance IQs on the WISC R with particular importance attributed to the discrepancies between verbal and performance scores. These hypotheses are based on the distinction between verbal and non-verbal abilities which is historically evidenced in factor analytic support and continues to be applicable for the WISC III.

Traditionally, the full-scale IQ (FSIQ) – the average of VIQ and PIQ – was used as an estimate of overall ability.

Before using the FSIQ score, the separate profiles must be analysed: are the verbal and performance scaled scores sufficiently similar to make the full-scale score clinically meaningful? If there are significant discrepancies between the verbal and performance sub-tests, the full-scale score, which is the average of two widely diverging sets of abilities, is rendered meaningless as an indicator of overall intelligence.

The individual sub-test scores in children and adults with developmental disorders show marked discrepancies. In one case the scaled scores obtained by a

12 year old boy with developmental dyspraxia ranged between 2 (Block design) and 17 (Similarities).

Wechsler Scale profiles for developmental disorders are characterised by specific strengths and weaknesses in identified sub-tests.

Dyslexia

It is suggested that between 5 and 10 per cent of preschool children have language impairment. This proportion varies in relation to geographical location. By school age this proportion has dropped to between 3 and 5 per cent and as those figures suggest, 50 to 60 per cent of preschool children with identified language difficulty continue to show evidence of impairment.

Many youngsters who are initially diagnosed at the preschool stage as having a language impairment are later classified as having a language difficulty or defined as being dyslexic. The definition of dyslexia as summarised by Kamhi (1992) is:

> Dyslexia is a developmental language disorder whose defining characteristic is a lifelong difficulty processing phonological information. This difficulty involves encoding, retrieving, and using phonological codes in memory as well as deficits in phonological awareness and speech production. The disorder, which is often genetically transmitted, is generally present at birth and persists throughout the lifespan. A prominent characteristic of the disorder is spoken and written language deficiencies.

The developmental pattern of children diagnosed as dyslexic follows a familiar sequence. As preschoolers, they have delays in language acquisition and when they transfer to full-time education and through primary school such children demonstrate deficiencies in phonological awareness, word recognition, spelling and writing competencies, as well as in reading comprehension. The understanding of complex sentences, i.e. receptive language, and the verbal communication of sequential directions are similarly impaired. As adults they may be able to read adequately, but continue to show phonological deficits in rapid naming tasks and in repeating phonologically complex words.

The ACID profile – a pattern of low scores on the Arithmetic, Coding, Information and Digit span sub-tests of the Wechsler Scales has been advanced as a means of differentiating children with dyslexia (Petrauskas and Rourke 1979; Joschko and Rourke 1985). There were significant differences between VIQ and PIQ scores, the verbal abilities being the most depressed.

Historically, developmental dyslexia was identified as presenting two clinically distinct subtypes: (Prifitera and Saklofske 1998):
- A pattern of test performance with average to above average performance IQ; a depressed verbal IQ; delayed onset of language; expressive language difficulties; phonological errors in reading; associated errors in spelling but competent visual-spatial abilities and normal eye movements.
- An average verbal IQ with a significantly depressed performance IQ. Right–left confusion was evident; mirror or inverted writing; spelling errors; finger agnosia;

spatial dysgraphia (poor handwriting, poor use of space); some visual errors in reading; a phonetic decoding strategy; faulty eye movement during reading but competent oral language abilities.

Rourke (1989, 1995) identified two types of learning difficulty: those with a Basic Phonological Processing Disorder (BPPD) were assessed as having lower verbal than performance IQs and those characterised as having Non-verbal Learning Disability (NLD) had lower performance IQs.

NLD was characterised by evidence of poor performance on tasks requiring visual-spatial organisation together with poor psycho-motor, tactile perceptual and conceptual skills and abilities. Assessment of verbal skills indicated that performance was in the average range.

Clearly the second dyslexia subtype (average VIQ with depressed PIQ) and NLD would now be identified as exhibiting characteristics of developmental dyspraxia.

Rourke *et al.* (1986) compared the performances of children identified with NLD and a group of adults with Wechsler VIQ > PIQ discrepancies. The patterns of age-related performances of the adults and the children identified through neuropsychometric assessment were almost identical. This is confirmed by my own findings (Portwood 1996, 1999) which are discussed later in this chapter.

Ozols and Rourke (1988) suggest that children with NLD develop a particular configuration of academic learning difficulties and severe psychosocial disturbance which becomes more evident over time: children with the NLD profile are usually described by parents as emotionally or behaviourally disturbed. In contrast, children with dyslexia are identified with behavioural difficulties at a much lower frequency. Rourke *et al.* (1986) suggest that for the dyslexic child something in 'addition' to psycholinguistic difficulty is necessary for disturbed psychosocial functioning to occur. The factors which influence behaviour might be:

• unrealistic demands on the child
• conflicts within the peer group
• difficulty with social competence
• problems with maturation.

Profiles of developmental dyspraxia

The Wechsler Scales measure the cognitive abilities of children from the age of three to adulthood. There is continuing debate about the reliability of instruments which measure these abilities in young children.

Usually a 'Developmental Checklist' forms the basis of the assessment of a child younger than school age i.e. under five, but this can often reflect the child's access to external influences rather than assess his 'potential'. A child who has not had access to a bike will not be able to pedal; a child who has not been encouraged to examine shapes and complete inset puzzles will not excel initially at fitting jigsaw pieces together; knowledge of colours is dependent on the child having had them named to him. In addition, developmental assessments rely heavily on spatial/ perceptual tasks as a means of assessing cognitive ability. This has serious disadvantages for the child with dyspraxia: instead of identifying 'specific' learning difficulties the outcome may be to produce a profile more indicative of generalised learning difficulties.

As the tasks in developmental assessments become increasingly complex they align more closely with those found in standardised intelligence tests like the WPPSI which offers a more detailed and accurate profile of abilities.

Analysis of data

Since 1988, I have completed 462 psychometric assessments using the Wechsler Scales. They were categorised as follows:
- 57 WPPSI – 41 male, 16 female, age range 3.2 years to 7.3 years
- 139 WISC R – 126 male, 13 female, age range 7.7 years to 15.3 years
- 239 WISC III – 211 male, 28 female, age range 6.2 years to 16.10 years
- 27 WAIS – 14 male, 13 female, age range 16 years to 31 years.

Note: The ratio of males to females in the WISC III sample is heavily biased because of the inclusion of results from the assessment of 69 juveniles (all male) at Deerbolt Young Offenders Institution (Portwood 1999).

The majority of cases in the adult sample were self-referrals and this accounts for the elevated female:male ratio.

Analysis of the results confirms that the Wechsler profile identifies specific weaknesses in four areas: Arithmetic; Digit span; Coding and Block design. If the magnitude of the weakness is greater in Coding and Block design than in Arithmetic and Digit span sub-tests the Performance IQ will be lower than the Verbal IQ. There were, however, many examples of the converse occurring where the Verbal IQ was most depressed.

The discrepancy model when the Performance IQ is lower than the Verbal IQ should not therefore be considered as a 'diagnosis' of dyspraxia: it is the individual sub-test profile which is significant, not the overall IQs.

The analysis of sub-test scores of completed WPPSI assessments shows the 'expected' profile and on average verbal scores are higher than performance. These results are based on a sample of 57 pupils: 41 boys and 16 girls.

Figure 5.2 shows the average scaled scores achieved in each sub-test. Although Arithmetic, Geometric design (Coding equivalent) and Block design are the most depressed scores, the verbal scores are on average higher and the performance scores lower in the WPPSI assessment when compared with the analysis of scores achieved in the WISC (see below).

Average scores achieved in the WPPSI: VIQ 99 PIQ 80
Average scores achieved in the WISC: VIQ 92 PIQ 85

There can be many explanations as to why the performance scores are more depressed in the younger child. It is probable that the motor component is more significant at this level, so that any test which involves eye–hand co-ordination and perceptual skills presents major problems.

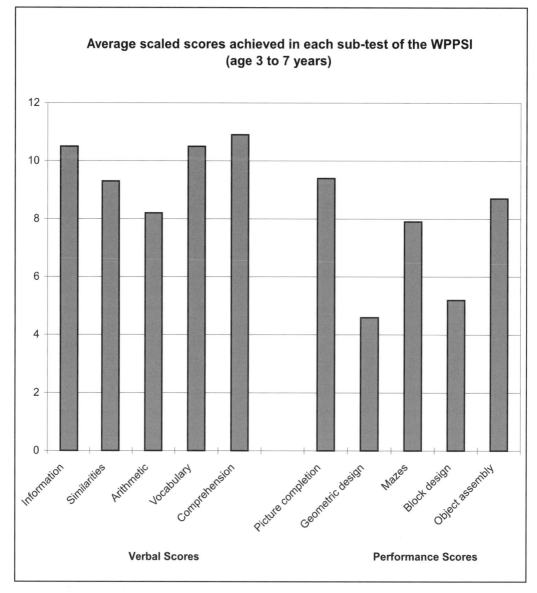

Figure 5.2 Average scaled scores achieved in each sub-test of the WPPSI

Verbal scores		Performance scores	
Information	10.5	Picture completion	9.4
Similarities	9.3	Geometric design	4.6
Arithmetic	8.2	Mazes	7.9
Vocabulary	10.5	Block design	5.2
Comprehension	10.9	Object assembly	8.7

Perhaps the two assessments WPPSI and WISC are measuring slightly different abilities.

Figure 5.3 shows the averaged scale scores achieved in each sub-test of the WISC. The sample comprises 378 pupils: 337 males and 41 females.

If the Arithmetic and Digit span sub-tests are excluded, the average of scaled scores = 9.79. If the Coding and Block design sub-tests are excluded, the average of summed performance scores = 9.9. The average of Arithmetic, Digit span, Coding and Block design sub-test scores = 5.71.

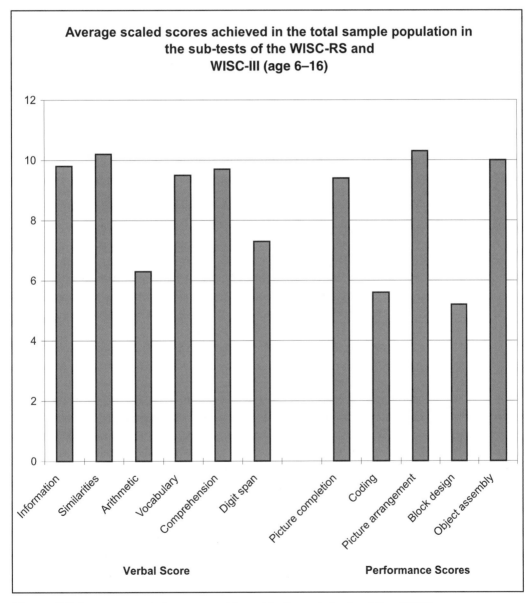

Figure 5.3 Average scaled scores achieved in the sub-tests of the WISC

Verbal scores		Performance scores	
Information	9.8	Picture completion	9.4
Similarities	10.2	Coding	5.6
Arithmetic	6.3	Picture arrangement	10.3
Vocabulary	9.5	Block design	5.2
Comprehension	9.7	Object assembly	10.0
Digit span	7.3		

When the results for pupils under the age of eight, assessed using the WISC, are analysed separately there are differences in some of the sub-test scores. Coding is higher but Picture completion and Object assembly significantly lower.

In this sub-sample there were 39 males and 8 females. The average scores achieved were:

Coding: 7.8
The nature of the coding task changes when the child reaches the age of eight and it is possible that the assessments are measuring slightly different capabilities.

Picture completion: 8.2
Limited concentration is more evident with younger pupils and this could affect the scores. If the child is unable to identify the missing feature quickly, he loses interest and wants to move on to the next card.

Object assembly: 8.7
The pieces reassemble to form pictures of a girl, horse, car, football and face. If the child is familiar with an object he will be more competent in reproducing it. Greater awareness of the environment could account for the improved scores in older pupils.

Pupil referral rates

The majority of youngsters were referred for assessment because concerns had been raised by parents or teachers about their school attainments and/or behaviour. The ratio of boys to girls differs in each age band. In the preschool and infants group (three to seven years) the ratio is approximately 3:1. When the children move into the junior classes and on to secondary education the ratio is much more heavily skewed towards the boys: approximately 8:1. The number of female adults with dyspraxia in further education is higher than males.

If we analyse specific reasons for referral in the early years (up to age seven), they include parents expressing concerns that their children have been slow to achieve some developmental milestones and are becoming isolated within their peer group. Problems with concentration, language development, poor co-ordination and delayed acquisition of social skills such as toileting and feeding are identified as major difficulties at this age, and the ratio of 3:1 is probably an accurate reflection of the incidence of dyspraxia. After the age of seven there is a greater need for boys to develop good motor skills to achieve acceptance within the peer group. Despite equal opportunities policies, observation still indicates that boys are more likely to engage in team games such as football, while girls prefer to spend time in smaller groups. Soon there are further displays of behavioural difficulties – the outlet of increasing frustration. Children who present behavioural problems in the classroom are quickly identified. The problems transfer to secondary education where truancy may become a major problem. Hence the ratio of 8:1 for this age group does not suggest that the dyspraxic proportion has changed but merely that boys are more likely to be identified.

So how can we explain differences in the referral rates of males and females after the age of 16? We may assume that a greater proportion of males are so disaffected with the 'system' that they do not consider further courses of study.

In the adult sample the profile of achievement differed significantly. This I attributed to the selection procedure which skewed the sample towards adults who in some cases had achieved academic success and were trying to access appropriate support services. Verbal skills were good and 82 per cent of those assessed were competent readers. Spelling presented problems in 68 per cent of cases and 77 per cent identified mental arithmetic as a major area of weakness.

Figure 5.4 is the psychometric profile obtained by the WAIS which highlighted strengths in many areas of verbal and non-verbal development. The sample population comprised 14 males and 13 females.

Average scores achieved in the WAIS: VIQ 99 PIQ 92.

In the adult sample there is little discrepancy between verbal and performance IQ. Individual sub-test scores identify improving ability in areas of greatest competence: verbal skills. Handwriting difficulties had been overcome by using word processors and the 'symptoms' of dyspraxia were in many cases disguised.

It is necessary to have some discussion regarding the use of the Wechsler Scales for the assessment of children and adolescents who show some evidence of neurological disease or disorder.

There are a number of types of paediatric neurological diseases and disorders wherein the dyspraxic pattern of neuropsychological strengths and weaknesses is very evident. These include: Williams Syndrome (Anderson and Rourke 1995); early hydrocephalus (Fletcher and Satz. 1983); Asperger's Syndrome (Klin *et al.* 1995) and congenital hypothyroidism (Rovet 1995). Their pattern of Wechsler Scale results exhibits specific strengths and weaknesses. Many of the studies of these forms of paediatric neuropathology use the Wechsler Scales to assist in diagnosis.

My own experience also identifies marked similarities in the profiles of children with Turner's Syndrome and Smith-Magensis Syndrome (SMS). Case studies of two youngsters – one with Turner's Syndrome, the other with Williams Syndrome – highlight the effectiveness of using the WISC assessment to identify specific strengths and weaknesses which ensures that intervention programmes best suited to their needs are available.

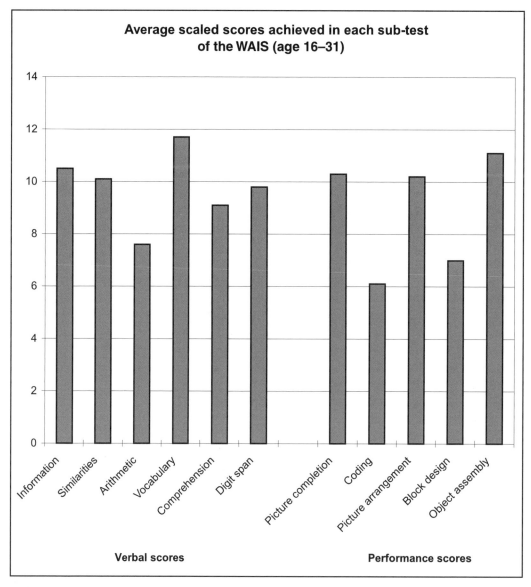

Figure 5.4 Average scaled scores achieved in each sub-test of the WAIS

Verbal scores		Performance scores	
Information	10.5	Picture completion	10.3
Similarities	10.1	Digit symbol (coding)	6.1
Arithmetic	7.6	Picture arrangement	10.2
Vocabulary	11.7	Block design	7.0
Comprehension	9.1	Object assembly	11.1
Digit span	9.8		

Case study: Elizabeth aged 10, with Turner's Syndrome

Elizabeth was induced at 38 weeks gestation. Labour was uneventful and the baby, who was delivered by forceps, weighed 6 lb. 2 oz. Although she was slightly jaundiced there were no concerns immediately after the birth.

Elizabeth had problems co-ordinating the movements required to suck and this was attributed to her 'high palate'. Feeding difficulties were reduced when, a week after birth, she transferred from breast to bottle milk and she began to gain weight as expected.

Elizabeth was an extremely irritable child from birth and sleeping problems persisted until she was two.

There were no concerns about Elizabeth's early development: she could sit unsupported at 7 months, pulled to stand at 12 months and walked independently at 14 months. She did not go through the crawling stage. Although Elizabeth was well into her second year before she could say single words, by the age of three she was speaking in sentences although some responses were stereotypical.

Elizabeth struggled to eat appropriately finding 'lumpy' food very difficult to swallow. By the age of two and a half concerns in relation to her growth forced investigation: she was diagnosed as having Turner's Syndrome.

Elizabeth is an extremely engaging youngster: she is lively, outgoing and has excellent verbal skills. She is a sensitive child not only in relation to herself but in being very aware of the needs of others. She makes constant demands on herself to produce school work of high quality. She is most anxious to please and is concerned to be liked by everyone. Her exceptional verbal competency had, in the past, masked many of the difficulties she was experiencing.

The Wechsler Profile (Figure 5.5) identified Elizabeth's strengths and weaknesses: the scores in the sub-tests ranged from 4 to 15. The variability in performance depended on the nature of the task. Tasks with a language bias were in the average to above average range. Tests with any visual/spatial orientation presented great difficulty to her. Elizabeth's VIQ was 119 and her PIQ 91: a difference of 28.

Problems were evident in the classroom when she was asked to reproduce and follow references for maps in geography or plot graphs in mathematics. Anything involving symmetry or motor-planning was virtually impossible.

The WISC Profile identified the target areas for intervention. Although Elizabeth was diagnosed with Turner's Syndrome she had the same perceptual and motor-planning difficulties as a youngster with dyspraxia. It is appropriate therefore to offer similar programmes of intervention which have been proven to be effective in developing the skills of children with dyspraxia. These programmes are discussed later.

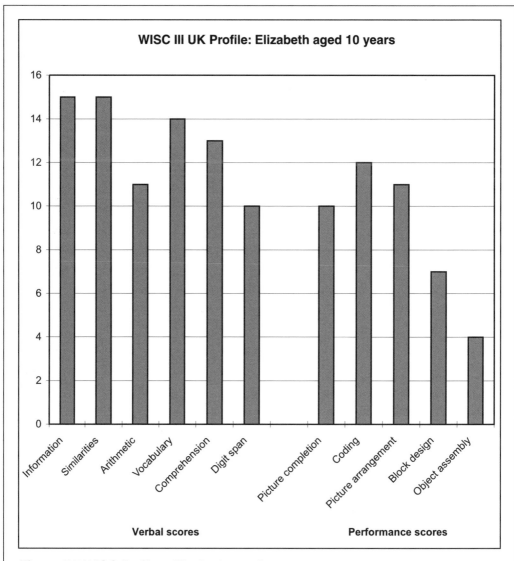

Figure 5.5 WISC Profile – Elizabeth, aged ten years

Verbal scores		**Performance scores**	
Information	15	Picture completion	10
Similarities	15	Coding	12
Arithmetic	11	Picture arrangement	11
Vocabulary	14	Block design	7
Comprehension	13	Object assembly	4
Digit span	10		

Case study: Andrew aged 13, with Williams Syndrome

Andrew had struggled throughout primary school although his verbal skills were recognised as an area of strength.

Andrew was born at 37 weeks and weighed 7 lb. 4 oz. He was the second child and his elder brother had required speech therapy. There was no evidence of early feeding difficulties and his parents' major concern was his poor concentration.

His early developmental history was unremarkable although some of the expected milestones were delayed.

On entry to reception class, Andrew could not identify any colours and he was seven before he developed an understanding of numbers to five. He was isolated in his peer group: he was not included in any activities unless the pupils were directed by the teacher. He was unco-ordinated and hated activities such as football: this was a serious disadvantage.

Although many of Andrew's presenting 'symptoms' suggested that he may have dyspraxia his developmental history did not follow the expected pattern.

Andrew's WISC Profile (Figure 5.6) identified strengths in his verbal ability and highlighted problems with auditory memory and perceptual/spatial awareness. His VIQ was 79 and PIQ 65. Andrew had been referred for a medical opinion and on transfer to secondary education was diagnosed as having Williams Syndrome.

Andrew was placed in a school where a group of pupils were identified as having dyspraxia. Structured lunchtime activities had been organised and he joined the 'gym' club. He was also provided with activities from the Frostig programme to improve his perceptual skills.

The following term, the progress of the pupils was evaluated. Andrew's motor skills had improved more than any other child's. His handwriting had become legible.

Providing a diagnosis is of little value if as educators we do not use the assessment information to offer a school/home based programme to improve a child's weaknesses and adapt the curriculum accordingly. Regardless of whether a child is diagnosed as dyspraxic, dyslexic or with a known genetic condition it is important to identify all the skills which can be improved through access to appropriate intervention.

Similarly, where there is evidence of comorbidity it is insufficient to address only the presenting symptoms of the 'primary' disorder.

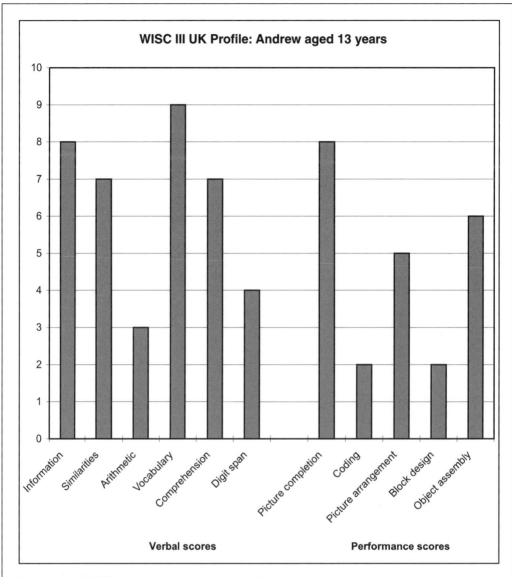

Figure 5.6 WISC Profile – Andrew, aged 13 years

Verbal scores		Performance scores	
Information	8	Picture completion	8
Similarities	7	Coding	2
Arithmetic	3	Picture arrangement	5
Vocabulary	9	Block design	2
Comprehension	7	Object assembly	6
Digit span	4		

Chapter 6

Parental observations and clinical assessment

Parents know their children better than anyone else and the parental interview is an essential part of the assessment. The session can be more focused if specific information is requested in the form of a questionnaire (Figure 6.1). The interview provides the necessary developmental history together with the parents' views of the child's difficulties, which may be very different from the perceptions of the teachers, who observe the child in a different environment. The parents will also have the opportunity to discuss the effect that the child's problems are having on the close and extended members of the family.

The developmental history often leads parents into a discussion about possible 'causes' and how some sort of 'blame' could be attributed to them, e.g. poor maternal diet; child fed on formula rather than breast milk; parent returned to work leaving child with nanny or in alternative day-care provision. Parents must be allowed the opportunity to discuss the frustration they have experienced, not only within themselves, feeling that they were in some way inadequate, but also from the lack of response they may have had from previous professionals who dismissed their concerns as 'over-anxiety'.

This interview facilitates the foundation of a diagnosis and identifies areas for further assessment. When the developmental history is complete the parents should be asked to describe the child as they see him now. What are their current concerns at home and, depending on the age of the child, in school?

Again questions can be structured to obtain information about the child's health, social/communication skills, behaviour, attainments, motor skills, hearing and vision (Figure 6.2). The same format can be presented to teachers for completion. If a youngster is of secondary age, impressions of a child's performance can vary significantly between subject teachers and members of the pastoral staff.

Parental Questionnaire

Background Information

Is X your first child? If not, what is his/her position in the family? ....

How old were you (mother) at the time of your child's birth? ....

Is there any family incidence of learning difficulty, eg dyslexia, dyspraxia, autistic spectrum disorder, ADHD or diagnosed genetic condition?

....

Is there any family incidence of allergy, eg food intolerance, eczema or asthma?

....

Is there a family history of coeliac disease?

....

Is there a family history of epilepsy or diabetes?

....

Is there any family incidence of depression or psychiatric illness?

....

Personal details

Can you remember whether you had any illness during your pregnancy?

....

Did nausea persist beyond the third month? ....

How did your weight progress? ....

When did you have your scan and was it repeated later during pregnancy?

....

Were there any concerns? ....

Was there anything unusual about the last trimester (6 - 9 months in utero)?

....

Figure 6.1 Parental questionnaire

Did you maintain a good diet? ....

Did you smoke during pregnancy? ....

Did you take any medication? ....

Were there any complications, eg eclampsia? ....

Birth details

At what stage of pregnancy was X delivered, eg 34 weeks, 42 weeks? ....

Was X induced and if so what was the method of delivery? ....

....

Was there any indication of foetal distress before the birth? ....

How long was the labour? Obtain additional information regarding the second stage if possible. ....

Were there any concerns immediately after the birth? ....

....

What was the birth weight? ....

Developmental profile

Child presentation

- Levels of activity (eg hyper-, hypo-active)

....

- Feeding - was weight gain appropriate? Any evidence of lactose intolerance?

....

- Sleeping - settled quickly or very irritable with very short periods of sleep?

....

- Was he/she a demanding child? ....

Figure 6.1 Parental questionnaire (continued)

Motor skills

- Sitting independently at ....

- Crawling at ....

- Walking independently at ....

Social skills

- Finger feeding at ....

- Co-ordinating a knife and fork at ....

- Toilet trained at ....

Language

- Made initial sounds (m, m- da, da) at ....

- Able to say 20+ distinguishable words at ....

- Used 3+ words to construct simple phrases at ....

Were there any other difficulties during the first 12 months?

Suggestions may be:

a) raised temperature/convulsion
b) jaundice
c) infections

....

....

....

Is there anything else you can remember that was of concern during this time?

....

....

....

Figure 6.1 Parental questionnaire (continued)

Later development

Hearing checked on ....

Vision checked on ....

Describe child's fine motor skills ....

....

Describe child's gross motor skills ....

....

Have there been any problems with health, eg eczema, asthma?

....

....

At what age and which immunisations have been given? ....

....

Is the child taking any regular medication? ....

....

Has the child had any additional assessment - paediatrician, speech therapist, physio/occupational therapist, optometrist, psychologist?

....

....

Do you have any additional information?

....

....

....

....

Figure 6.1 Parental questionnaire (continued)

Current information record form

Name................................. DOB .... School ....

Address ....

Contact number ....

Responses to questions provided by : (name) ....

Designation : (e.g. Parent/ teacher) ....

General Health

Are there any concerns about recurring problems e.g. Ear/ chest infections?

....

....

What illnesses has the child had e.g. Measles, chicken pox?

....

....

Has he/ she gained weight as expected and are there any dietary concerns?

....

Does he/ she have any allergies? ....

Social Skills

How does he/ she relate to family members? ....

....

How does he/ she relate to children in school? ....

....

What are his/ her main interests? ....

....

Does he/ she have any particular habits or repetitive behaviours? ....

....

How does he/ she cope in unfamiliar settings? ....

....

Figure 6.2 Current information record form

Behaviour

How does he/ she respond to being directed? ....

....

Is concentration (time on task) appropriate for his/ her age? ....

....

How does he/ she respond to praise? ....

....

How does he/ she respond to sanctions? ....

....

Are there any other behaviours which concern you? ....

....

Does he/ she show heightened emotions in some situations e.g. Very excitable, anxious, sad? - please give examples ....

....

Is there any evidence of 'handflapping' when excited? ....

Hearing/ Vision

Hearing checked : Date .... Outcome ....
Vision checked : Date .... Outcome ....

Communication skills

Were there any concerns regarding language development e.g. Delayed acquisition, problems with articulation? ....

....

Was he/ she referred to a speech therapist?   Yes/No
Date .... Outcome .... Therapist ....

Does he/ she follow instructions appropriately? ....

....

Does he/ she answer questions appropriately? ....
Are there any current concerns? ....

....

Figure 6.2 Current information record form (continued)

Motor-skills

At what age did he/ she develop the following skills?

Skill	Age
Walking independently	....
Jumping	....
Running	....
Hopping	....
Riding a bike	....

Completing a simple 4 piece inset puzzle	....
Threading beads	....
Holding a crayon/ pencil	....

Copying a shape e.g. , **O** **+**	....
Draw recognisable figures	....

Pulling a zip fastener	....
Fastening a button	....
Co-ordinating a knife and fork	....
Writing legibly	....

Attainments

Assessment of reading:

Test	Date	C.A	Score

Assessment of spelling:

Test	Date	C.A	Score

Figure 6.2 Current information record form (continued)

Assessment of comprehension:

Test	Date	C.A	Score

Assessment of numeracy skills

Test	Date	C.A	Score

Additional information e.g. Baseline Assessment, SAT's, Cognitive assessment

....
....
....
....
....
....
....
....
....
....
....
....
....
....
....
....
....
....
....

Figure 6.2 Current information record form (continued)

Health visitor assessment

The health visitor is the professional with whom the parent and child are most likely to be involved prior to starting school. The health visitor undertakes developmental assessments of children up to the age of three and plays a key role in identifying those who are experiencing difficulty achieving the expected milestones. The parent may have concerns about areas of the child's development which, if considered in isolation, could be dealt with by accepting that children develop at different rates. However, when there are a number of factors which suggest that skills are being acquired at a significantly slower rate than would be expected for his/her age, structured intervention can be beneficial.

The health visitor will suggest strategies to the parent to improve the development of particular skills and she may refer to the GP for further assessment. This could result in referral to a Child Development Team which usually comprises a paediatrician, physio/occupational therapist, speech therapist, psychologist, health visitor, representative from the local education authority and anyone else closely involved with the child. The role of the Child Development Team is discussed in the next chapter in relation to the responsibilities of Health and Education in identifying and supporting children with special educational needs.

Referral to this multidisciplinary team offers the child the best opportunity for assessment by specialists in all areas of child development. Unfortunately the incidence of dyspraxia (between 2 per cent and 5 per cent of the population) suggests that that there will probably be at least one dyspraxic child in every classroom. The vast majority will not have been identified before starting school and an even smaller proportion will be referred to outside specialists.

Teachers and those working with the pupils on a daily basis are best placed to acknowledge the child's difficulties and work with parents to identify skills which can be improved by targeted programmes of intervention. School-based assessment will be discussed later in this chapter.

Where outside specialists have been involved, they are able to provide parents and teachers with information about the child's strengths and weaknesses and offer strategies to improve where possible the areas of greatest concern.

Speech therapy assessment – identification of verbal dyspraxia

Many youngsters who are diagnosed by the age of three with developmental dyspraxia have been referred by the speech therapist. Youngsters with dyspraxia, in just over 50 per cent of the cases, have problems with the acquisition of language skills and their difficulties are evident mainly in expressive rather than receptive language.

In the sample population of 62 youngsters under the age of seven referred for assessment between 1991 and 1997, 24 had significant problems articulating speech sounds.

The developmental history of the majority of these youngsters identified feeding problems virtually from birth. Some had not developed the appropriate 'sucking reflex' and consequently breast feeding was unsuccessful. Bottle feeding appeared preferable. There were also major difficulties when the child transferred from milk to solid foods. Co-ordinating the tongue was problematic and the children continued to 'choke' on lumpy food. This established a pattern of eating where preference was always given to virtually 'pureed' food and 'snack foods' such as crisps and puffed wheat which dissolves very quickly. One parent reported that their child had followed a diet consisting almost exclusively of custard and prawn crackers between the ages of two and five.

Children with verbal dyspraxia find it difficult to co-ordinate the 'speech apparatus' used to produce sounds. This consists of:

- the lips
- the tongue
- the soft palate
- the larynx
- the jaw.

Youngsters with developmental verbal dyspraxia experience difficulty sequencing the voluntary movements of this apparatus to produce comprehensible sounds.

The diagnosis of developmental verbal dyspraxia (DVD) where there are no other symptoms of dyspraxia, i.e. generalised difficulties with gross and fine motor co-ordination and perceptual skills, can be problematic as there is some expectation that access to appropriate intervention programmes to improve co-ordination and perceptual skills will facilitate the improvement of speech.

In many instances there is a family history of delayed development of speech. Generally the child's comprehension of language is age-appropriate but the delayed onset of speech sounds makes verbal communication very difficult and the children can become isolated within their peer group from a very early age, often in the playgroup or nursery.

Characteristically the child will have been late developing a single-word vocabulary, often after the age of three. Attempts at verbal communication have been met with little response and gestures become a major feature of social interaction. The child has difficulty not only in articulating sounds but also in placing the sounds in the correct sequence. The letter sequence within words and the word sequence itself are often muddled. Children learn very quickly that because of articulation difficulties their speech is indistinct and other children and some adults are unable to comprehend the meaning of their words. The child soon discovers that rather than receiving encouragement to talk he/she is being criticised: this compounds the problem.

Access to appropriate therapy offered by a language specialist encourages the child to improve the skills necessary to co-ordinate the production of speech sounds. However, there is evidence from my own research that the developmental difficulties persist until the ages of seven and a half to eight and a half and until that time, for some youngsters, even with high levels of specialist input, very little improvement is evident.

The Nuffield Hearing and Speech Centre have developed a programme designed specifically for children aged three to seven with verbal dyspraxia. It offers a structured approach to therapy and in contrast to my own observations the team at the Royal National Throat, Nose and Ear Hospital in London who developed the programme report significant improvements in language skills even with much younger children. More information is available from the Principal Speech and Language therapists at the Nuffield Centre RNTNE Hospital.

Children with such articulation disorders with whom I have been involved appear to gain most from an intensive course of speech therapy at around the age of seven to seven and a half when the benefits are evident very quickly.

Where a child displays the symptoms of verbal dyspraxia as part of a wider condition it is important to offer appropriate programmes of intervention to address all the areas of difficulty. Youngsters can derive a great deal of benefit if programmes can be implemented within the mainstream classroom environment, especially if they can be integrated into everyday curricular activities.

An understanding that the child's communication difficulties will improve significantly with maturity enables parents and teachers to ensure that the child is included within the peer group and does not become socially isolated before effective verbal communication skills are established.

Language development is a crucial part of assessing whether the child shows signs of general immaturity or a language disorder: youngsters with developmental dyspraxia have delayed, not disordered, language acquisition.

Assessment of the acquisition of language skills is fundamental in determining the differential diagnosis between autistic spectrum disorders and those such as dyspraxia, dyslexia and ADHD where language is affected. Figure 6.3 shows the development of speech and language alongside the developmental sequence of sounds. Assessment of the child's language skills would determine whether the child is acquiring the skills in the appropriate sequence, albeit more slowly, or whether the language itself is disordered.

Age	Development of speech and language	Sounds
0-3 months	Cries and makes other vocalisations: gurgles – 'shouts'	
3–6 months	Makes 2+ speech sounds 'ooh', 'aah'	
6–9 months	Babbles 4+ syllables	
9–12 months	Says 'Mama', 'Dada'. Uses gestures – shakes head for 'yes' and 'no'	
12–18 months	Recognises own name, babbles tunefully, likes rhymes and jingles, uses 20+ clear words and responds to simple requests with gestures (pointing) 'Where is the ball?'	'm' 'd' 'b'
18–24 months	Vocabulary 50+ words, understands simple sentences, names given objects, e.g. car, doll, cup	'n' 'w' 't' 'p'
2–3 years	Can repeat and talks in sentences of 6+ syllables e.g. 'My cat is black and white'. Uses 2+ descriptive words 'big' 'hot', prepositions 'in', 'on'	'h' 's' 'y' 'i' 'k' 'h' 'ing'
3–4 years	Takes turns to speak in conversation, uses 2+ personal pronouns – 'my', 'his', knows 3+ colours. Consistently uses plurals	'z' 'sh' 'ch' 'j' 'f' 'v'
4–5 years	Speech intelligible, although some 'th', 'u', 'r' confusion. Uses sentences of 10+ syllables e.g. 'I go to school in the car with my Dad'. Pronouns and tense used appropriately.	'th' 'r'

Figure 6.3 Development of speech and language

The speech therapist is often a primary source of referral to the Child Development Team or other specialists. The majority of preschool children referred to me for assessment of dyspraxia come via this route.

The responsibility for obtaining the developmental history depends on the route of the referral. In the case of a preschool child it is the Health Authority which identifies youngsters with special educational needs. When the child enters the education system the school staff have a responsibility to the child. Assessment therefore can take place in either the health or the educational setting but it is crucial that cooperative working practices are in place to ensure the best possible outcome for the child.

Physio/occcupational therapy assessment

The therapist will undertake an observational assessment and may use a variety of standardised tests. They assess not only motor function but also perceptual skills and can determine whether delays in these areas are significant or whether they will improve with maturity. The titles of some of these standardised assessments include:

- Bruininks Oseretsky
- T.O.M.I. (Test of Motor Impairment)
- S.I.P.T. (Sensory Integration and Praxis Test).

When a child has generalised developmental delay it would be expected that language, self-help, cognition and motor skills would all be affected. It is important to determine whether motor and perceptual skills are significantly depressed in relation to other areas of development. Lee and French (1997) in their 'Handbook for Therapists' identify specific areas for testing:

- Muscle tone
  - Determine whether they are hyper/hypotonic.
- Shoulder stability
  - Assessment of the child's strength, reaching and grasping mechanism and weight-bearing ability.
- Hip stability
  - Ability of the child to distribute weight appropriately between upper and lower limbs. Adequate strength around the hips is necessary to maintain good balance.
- Active extension
  - Can the child lift all four limbs simultaneously when lying on his stomach?
- Rotation
  - Can the child roll from side to side and across a distance of 10+ metres? Many parents of dyspraxic children report observing difficulties during the first year of development with this activity.
- Eye–hand/eye–foot co-ordination
  - Can the child throw, kick and balance a ball between hands?
  - Is the child able to copy a series of specified shapes?

- Midline crossing
  - Does the child complete activities on the right side of the body with the right hand and vice versa or can the child extend and touch opposite sides of the body, e.g. left ear with right hand?
- Directional/spatial awareness
  - Can the child move forwards, backwards and sideways appropriately?
  - Can the child judge distances or is he/she constantly bumping into objects, or tripping over?
- Symmetrical/bilateral integration
  - Ability to stop between sequential movements, e.g. hop, skip and jump.
- Laterality
  - Does the child consistently use the same hand for directed activities, e.g. writing, catching?
  - Assess foot dominance, e.g. ask child to hop.
  - Assess eye dominance, e.g. ask child to look through a 'telescope' at an object or fixed point.

They go on to discuss the appropriateness of specific treatment methods and the results are discussed in the Journal *Physiotherapy* (Lee and Smith 1998). Advice may be given to parents and teachers about posture and programmes of intervention may be delivered in a clinical setting or the school/home environment.

High levels of anxiety often lead to excessive tiredness and this affects muscular control. Poor posture is often a feature of dyspraxia and advice may be required regarding seating position.

The child may have additional problems caused by an abnormal pen-grip. The occupational therapist will be able to assess whether a large-barrelled textured pen or one with a triangular grip is beneficial. A sloping work-surface may be recommended.

Some therapists have undertaken further postgraduate specialist training in Sensory Integration Therapy (Ayres 1972). A special sensory environment is created and although it is not appropriate for all children, many show significant improvement after therapy.

Access to appropriate movement programmes has proved to be extremely effective for youngsters with dyspraxia. It is not only their co-ordination which improves but also handwriting, concentration, self-esteem and behaviour (Portwood 1996, 1999).

Optometric assessment – identification of ocular-motor dyspraxia

Optometric assessment has proved a valuable tool in providing detailed information about the impact of restricted visual functioning in specific learning difficulties. A great deal of research has been carried out to determine whether filters and tinted lenses bring about improvements in the reading capabilities of dyslexic youngsters and adults. More recently, optometric assessment has been invaluable in determining whether ocular-motor movement, in particular, affects the learning capabilities of youngsters with dyspraxia.

Diagnosis of specific learning difficulties dyslexia/dyspraxia is heavily reliant on the information provided by psychometric assessment, but in addition to identifiable psychometric profiles there are also optometric correlations.

Aetiology

There is some evidence to suggest that there may be slight abnormalities in the cerebral organisation in dyslexia and dyspraxia and there may be subtle lesions in several focal sites, predominantly in the left cerebral cortex. Research literature suggests that there may be specific eye problems which occur more often in youngsters with specific learning difficulties.

Assessing the level of difficulty

Many youngsters with dyspraxia have ocular-motor instability. This affects tracking, i.e. movement of the eye appropriately from left to right which is necessary to follow the words on a line or indeed sequence the letters in a word. There may be additional problems with focusing.

The optometrist would test for *hypermetropia* (long-sightedness) where the eyeball is too short for the power of the lens and the image of a distant or near object is focused behind the retina. *Myopia* results when the eyeball is too long for the power of the lens and the image is focused in front of the retina. This is usually a problem with distance and not near-vision. *Astigmatism* is where the curvature of the cornea in one meridian is different from that 90° to it. This means that instead of a sharp, pin-point image on the retina the individual experiences a 'blur circle'. This would appear, for example, if when looking at the letter 'T' the horizontal bar was either more or less clear than the vertical bar. These refractive errors can be corrected with spectacles.

Many youngsters with dyspraxia have problems with *accommodation* which is an inability to focus on near tasks. A reduced amplitude of *accommodation* has been found to be unusually common in youngsters with specific learning difficulties. This can be a particular problem when children are tired as they have problems maintaining words in focus.

Symptoms of accommodation disorders

- sore eyes
- rapid blinking
- constantly changing working distances
- vertical ghosting
- continually losing position on the page
- lack of attention
- distance blur after working on near tasks
- eye rubbing

- variable eye/hand performance
- near-work avoidance.
    Three specific areas are examined:
    1. **Amplitude of accommodation:** This is the ability to change the shape of the lens within the eye to view near tasks.
    2. **Accommodative lag:** This examination is to ensure that the child is able to focus on the plane of the words on the page of the book that they are viewing. Many youngsters with ocular-motor difficulties tend to focus behind the page and not actually on the words.
    3. **Accommodative facility:** This is the ability of the eyes to relax and concentrate on focusing. This is most important when children look at the blackboard and then refocus on the page of the book in front of them.

Convergence

When reading text it is important not just to focus but also converge, i.e. align eyes, on the words being read. A reduced amplitude of convergence is frequently associated with specific learning difficulties. If difficulties are identified, the optometrist can suggest specific exercises to improve the efficiency of the system.

Binocular vision

Binocular vision means that both eyes work together so the brain can produce a three-dimensional image. Binocular instability is an area which should be examined where there are ocular-motor problems.

One of the most common binocular dysfunctions is an over-convergence of the eyes for near tasks. This is called *convergence excess* and it is often connected with a convergence to accommodation ratio. For example: imagine you are looking at the word CAT. It would be expected that the focus would be to the middle of the word, i.e. both eyes focus on the letter A at the centre. What is often evident in youngsters with over-convergence problems is that the right eye looks at the letter C at the start of the word and the left eye looks at the letter T at the end. This causes great problems with reading and writing and can often explain the reversals evident when the child is heard reading aloud or by examination of a handwriting sample.

This condition can be treated with low-powered reading lenses.

The importance of ocular-motor control

During the process of reading and writing the eyes proceed along the letter sequence in a series of step-like movements known as saccades. These are separated by fixation pauses. During this pause information is acquired from the relevant section of text. The width of this section, normally measured by the number of letters, is termed the *'perceptual span'*. At the end of the line the eyes make a large saccade or 'return sweep'. Most of the other saccades are in the left to right direction. Occasionally one is made in the opposite direction to return to previously read text and these are called regressions.

Many youngsters with dyspraxia, although they are competent when assessed on their ability to 'read' individual words, experience a 'system' breakdown when required to read text. This has an enormous effect on fluency and when this breaks down there is evidence of increased anxiety, which in turn reduces the child's ability to read, particularly if he is expected to do so in front of the whole class.

Using coloured overlays and precision tints

The use of colour, either in the form of overlays or tinted lenses to help those with reading problems, has been in evidence for some time.

In 1980, Olive Meares, a special needs teacher in New Zealand, presented a paper on the perceptual distortions experienced by some children while reading and how, in some cases, these distortions were ameliorated by the use of coloured overlays. Three years later Helen Irlen, an American psychologist, reported that she had found adults with reading difficulties became more competent when the print was covered with a transparent coloured sheet. She labelled the condition 'Scotopic Sensitivity Syndrome'.

Over the years there has been a great deal of controversy over therapeutic use of colour for those experiencing reading difficulties. There are a number of possible explanations as to why tinted lenses and coloured overlays improve reading skills. One explanation suggests that there is a reduction in 'pattern glare'. This is where the person reading the text interprets it as running into a long thick black line rather than seeing it as individual words.

Pattern glare is dependent on:
- Space between the lines of text
- The degree of contrast between the print and the background
- The colour of the text
- The level of light intensity
- The origination of the text in relation to the observer, i.e. the pattern glare may change if the page is rotated through 45°.

Overlays should be given only to those who show sustained benefit from using them. Youngsters who have benefited from coloured overlays state that they reduce the perceptual distortions of the text. The youngsters also reported that they were able to read text more fluently with less discomfort and fewer headaches.

There continues to be great debate regarding the effect of visual problems and their relation with specific learning difficulties. There is no doubt that for some youngsters access to a specific programme to improve the focus and movement of the eyes has brought about remarkable results.

School-based assessment

Staff will be aware that there are discrepancies between the child's ability to provide information verbally and his/her ability to record it manually. There will be evidence of perceptual problems and organisational difficulties. Many of the characteristics of dyspraxic youngsters described in Chapter 4 will be apparent. The majority of children and adults with dyspraxia are never referred to external specialists. With limited resources the problems experienced by many youngsters are not severe enough to warrant such attention. However, it is these youngsters who are 'just failing' for whom identification and intervention – and a great deal of good-will on the part of the staff – has proved most successful.

To facilitate identification I have developed a Motor Skills Screening (Figure 6.5) and the proforma (Figure 6.4) enables the assessor to record the behaviours observed during assessment. The Motor Skills Screening is designed for use with pupils from Key Stage 2 to adulthood.

There are ten activities and the assessor should observe and record associated movements and other physical signs such as tremors or tongue-thrusting. The behaviours illustrated indicate a motor difficulty. For a more detailed explanation on the use of this test and subsequent intervention, reference should be made to: *Developmental Dyspraxia – Identification and Intervention* (Portwood 1999).

Where there is evidence of a motor problem the entry point to the intervention programme is then determined by completing a 'baseline motor assessment' (this is referred to in Chapter 9, and a proforma is given in Figure 9.1).

Supplementary information, which would include any standardised assessments in literacy or numeracy, should be considered when producing the child's individual education plan.

The most successful outcomes are achieved when children with difficulties are identified at an early stage in their development and appropriate resources from Health and Education are made available to them. It would appear that cooperative working relationships are available in most areas for the preschool child: beyond that, services become less accessible. Perhaps in the future this will not be the case if some consideration is given to the 'systems' currently operating within the Health and Education Authorities which could facilitate the setting up of a multidisciplinary assessment team for older pupils and adults.

Motor Skills Screening		
Name................................. Date............................ Age.......................................		
Activity	**Behaviour**	**Date**
1. Walking on toes forwards and backwards		
2. Walking on heels forwards and backwards		
3. Walking on insides of feet		
4. Walking on outsides of feet		
5. Recognising fingers touched when obscured from view. Right hand then left		
6. Finger sequencing – right then left		
7. Wrist rotation		
8. Balancing on each foot		
9. Touching end of nose with index finger of each hand (eyes closed)		
10. Jumping: feet together		

Figure 6.4 Motor skills screening proforma

Activity

1.   Walking on toes

Behaviour

Arms move outwards and hands bend at the wrist away from the body

Activity

2.   Walking on heels

Behaviour

Arms held upwards from the elbow, hands bend upwards towards the body

Activity

3.   Walking on insides of feet

Behaviour

Arms extended behind, hands bend turning away from the body

Figure 6.5 Motor skills screening assessment

Activity

4.   Walking on outsides of feet

Behaviour

Arms bend outwards and wrists turn in

Activity

5.   Obscure one of the child's hands. The examiner touches two of the child's hidden fingers simultaneously. Ask the child to point out (with the other hand) those touched

Record 5 times with each hand

Behaviour

The child is consistently unable to identify the correct fingers

Figure 6.5 Motor skills screening assessment (continued)

Activity

6.   Ask the child to sequence each finger against the thumb of the same hand, slowly at first, then more quickly. Test each hand separately, then try hands together

Behaviour

Look for associated movements with the relaxed hand. Usually the child mirrors the activity

Activity

7. Demonstrate and ask the child to rotate both wrists simultaneously with the thumbs moving towards and then away from each other

Behaviour

See whether the child can rotate his wrists without his elbows moving outwards

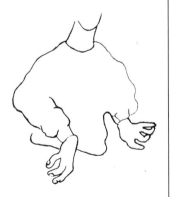

Figure 6.5 Motor skills screening assessment (continued)

Activity

8.   Ask the child to balance on each foot

Behaviour

The child should be able to achieve 10+
seconds on each foot

Activity

9.   Demonstrate by standing in front of
the child. Make a wide arc first with the
right hand and then the left, and touch the
end of your nose with the index finger of
each. Make sure that eyes are closed

Behaviour

Child will probably distract the examiner
by coughing at the last minute or will
touch his nose with the whole of his hand

Activity

10.   Ask the child to jump repeatedly
with feet together

Behaviour
Problems will be observed in establishing
the jumping routine. Elbows held tightly
into waist, arms upwards and fists
clenched

Figure 6.5 Motor skills screening assessment (continued)

Chapter 7

The role of the Education and Health Authorities in identifying and making provision for children with special educational needs

The 1944 Education Act formed the basis for all subsequent legislation. In the 1970s there were increasing concerns among educators that the 1944 Act gave parents very limited rights to have their opinion considered and the identification and subsequent treatment of children was based on a medical model of diagnosis.

In 1974 the Warnock Committee was established by the Secretary of State for Education and Science to:

> Review the educational provision in England, Wales and Scotland for children and young people handicapped by disabilities of body and mind, taking into account the medical aspects of their needs together with arrangements to prepare them for entry into employment and to consider the most effective use of resources for these purposes.

In 1978 the Warnock Report published its recommendations:
- It should be acknowledged that up to 20 per cent of children would have learning difficulties at some time
- The idea of a 'continuum of special needs' replaced the 'categorisation' of children
- These categories would instead be identified as learning difficulties for which there would be educational provision
- Parents would have an active role and would work in partnership with all those involved in the assessment
- A named person should be appointed to support the parents of children with special needs
- Wherever possible, children with learning difficulties should be educated in mainstream schools
- Children identified as requiring support over and above that which was normally available in school should have a record of needs
- Pupils' needs should be reassessed two years before their school-leaving date

- Teacher training courses should include instruction on the identification of and provision for children with special educational needs
- In-service training should be provided for existing teachers and advisory and support services should be extended
- Cooperative working arrangements between education, health and social services should be improved. A named doctor and nurse should be appointed for each special school. Appropriate resources should be made available by Health Authorities to develop effective child health services in schools
- Social Services should appoint a liaison officer to link with the Careers Advisory Service
- The planning and delivery of services for children and young people with special educational needs should be better co-ordinated
- Voluntary organisations should have a greater role in the provision of services.

There have been many changes in the way education authorities make provision for youngsters with special educational needs since the publication of the Warnock Report and this became legislation in the 1981 Education Act.

The Warnock Report had identified that as many as 20 per cent of school pupils would at some time have special educational needs and the 1981 Act suggested that 2 per cent of the pupils would have needs that were sufficient to require additional provision. The 1981 Education Act placed upon Local Education Authorities a *duty* to identify, assess and determine appropriate provision for children with special educational needs. This provision was to be made in mainstream schools with the following conditions:

- The parents' views had to be considered
- Children should receive the provision most appropriate for their learning difficulties
- The provision must be compatible with the efficient education of other children in the class/school
- The provision must be an efficient use of resources.

The 1993 Education Act was a development of the legislation framework of the 1981 Act and it was followed by the 1996 Education (Consolidation) Act.

The *Code of Practice* issued by the Secretary of State for Education in 1994 gives guidance to LEAs in respect of their responsibilities identified in the 1993 Education Act.

Identification and assessment of special educational needs

The term 'special needs' can be defined under three headings:

1. Learning Difficulty

A child has a learning difficulty if he/she:

- Has significantly greater difficulty in learning than the majority of children of his/her age
- Has a disability which either prevents or hinders him/her from making use of

educational facilities of a kind provided for children of the same age in schools within the area of the Local Education Authority concerned
- Is aged under five and falls into one of these categories, or is likely to do so later, if special educational provision is not made.

2. Special Educational Provision
- For children under two this means any educational provision.
- For children over two, this means educational provision that is additional to, or otherwise different from, the educational provision made generally for children of similar age in schools maintained by the Local Education Authority concerned.

3. Special Educational Needs
- A child has special educational needs if he/she has a learning difficulty that calls for special educational provision to be made.
- The *Code of Practice* requires schools to introduce 'Stage procedures' for the identification of children with special educational needs.
- The *Code of Practice* also states that the special educational needs of the great majority of children should be met effectively within the school's own resources, without the statutory involvement of the Local Education Authority. In a minority of cases, perhaps two per cent of children, the Local Education Authority will need to make a Statutory Assessment of special educational needs.

Statutory assessment

There are specified procedures that the LEA must follow to make provision for a child with special educational needs. The procedures if the child is in LEA provision require an assessment under Section 323 of the 1996 Act.

Section 165(3) of the 1993 Act identifies the LEA in which the child is resident as having responsibility where he/she is educated within the independent sector if they have been brought to the LEA's attention as having or probably having special educational needs. Parents have the right to request an assessment under Section 329 of the 1996 Act.

The assessment process, after obtaining the views of parents, requires written advice from:
- A qualified teacher who has detailed knowledge of the child
- An educational psychologist
- A designated medical officer (e.g. school doctor, paediatrician)

In addition, other professionals working with the child e.g. speech therapist, physio/occupational therapist or child psychiatrist will be asked to contribute information.

'Statement' of special educational needs

When the written advice from parents and the professionals involved is submitted the LEA determine whether they will issue a 'Statement'. Practice varies widely between Educational Authorities and depends on the LEA policy on the type of provision allocated through Statements and the resources generally available in mainstream schools. When comparisons are made between LEAs it is evident that some children receive high levels of additional resourcing without a Statement while in other areas support is totally dependent on having one issued.

Whether or not a Statement is issued, the Education and Health authorities share the responsibility for identifying children with special educational needs.

The *Code of Practice* identifies seven areas of special educational needs, as follows.

1. Learning difficulties

Some children with learning difficulties will be identified before school age and the majority should be identified very early in their school careers. Their general level of academic attainment will be significantly below that of their peers. In most cases they will have difficulty in acquiring basic literacy and numeracy skills and many will have significant speech and language difficulties. Some will also have poor social skills and may show signs of emotional and behavioural difficulties.

Where children have severe or profound and multiple learning difficulties, the LEA will be able to draw upon a considerable body of existing knowledge arising from assessments and provision made by child health and social services, which may have been involved with children and families from a very early stage. Many children with severe or profound and multiple difficulties will have additional secondary disabilities and assessment arrangements will need to take account of the possibility of such disabilities. (Section 3:56 *Code of Practice*, 1994.)

2. Specific learning difficulties (e.g. developmental dyspraxia)

Some children may have significant difficulties in reading, writing, spelling or manipulating numbers which are not typical of their general level of performance. They may gain some skills in some subjects quickly and demonstrate a high level of ability orally, yet may encounter sustained difficulty in gaining literacy or numeracy skills. Such children can become severely frustrated and may also have emotional and/or behavioural difficulties. (Section 3:60 *Code of Practice*, 1994.)

3. Emotional and behavioural difficulties

Emotional and behavioural difficulties may result, for example, from abuse or neglect; physical or mental illness; sensory or physical impairment; or psychological trauma. In some cases emotional and behavioural difficulties may arise or be exacerbated by circumstances within the school environment. They may also be associated with other learning difficulties. (Section 3:65 *Code of Practice*, 1994.)

Emotional and behavioural difficulties may become apparent in a wide variety of forms – including withdrawn, depressive or suicidal attitudes; obsessional preoccupation with eating habits; school phobia; substance misuse; disruptive, antisocial and uncooperative behaviour; and frustration, anger and threat or actual violence. (Section 3:67 *Code of Practice*, 1994.)

4. Physical difficulties

A child's physical difficulties may be the result of an illness or injury, which might have short- or long-term consequences, or may arise from a congenital condition. Such difficulties may, without any action by the school or the LEA, limit the child's access to the full curriculum. Some children with physical disabilities may also have sensory impairments, neurological problems and learning difficulties. (Section 3:71 *Code of Practice*, 1994.)

5. Medical conditions

Some medical conditions may, if appropriate action is not taken, have a significant impact on the child's academic attainment and/or may give rise to emotional and behavioural difficulties. Some of the commonest medical conditions are likely to be congenital heart disease, epilepsy, asthma, cystic fibrosis, haemophilia, sickle cell anaemia, diabetes, renal failure, eczema, rheumatoid disorders and leukaemia and childhood cancers.

These conditions may in themselves significantly impair the child's ability to participate fully in the curriculum and the wide range of activities in school. Some medical conditions will affect the child's progress and performance intermittently, others on a continuous basis throughout the child's school career. (Sections 3:89 & 3:90 *Code of Practice*, 1994.)

6. Sensory difficulties

1) Hearing

A significant proportion of children may have some degree of hearing difficulty. Hearing losses may be temporary or permanent. Temporary hearing losses are actually caused by the condition known as 'glue ear' and occur most often in the early years. Such hearing losses fluctuate and may be mild or moderate in degree. They can seriously compound other learning difficulties. Schools should be alert to such evidence as persistently discharging ears.

Permanent hearing losses are usually sensori-neural and vary from mild through moderate to severe or profound. Children with severe or profound hearing loss may have severe or complex communication difficulties. (Sections 3:75 & 3:76 *Code of Practice*, 1994.)

2) Vision

Visual difficulties take many forms with widely differing implications for a child's education. They range from relatively minor and correctable conditions to total blindness. Some children are born blind; others lose their sight, partially or completely, as a result of accidents or illness. In some cases visual impairment is one aspect of multiple disability. Whatever the cause of the child's visual impairment, the major issue in identifying and assessing the child's special educational needs will relate to the degree and nature of functional vision, partial sight or blindness, and the child's ability to adapt socially and psychologically as well as to progress in an educational context. (Section 3:81 *Code of Practice*, 1994.)

7. *Speech and language (communication) difficulties*

Although most speech and language difficulties will have been identified before a child reaches school, some children will continue to have significant speech and language difficulties which impair their ability to participate in the classroom when they start school. This in turn may have serious consequences for the child's academic attainment and also give rise to emotional and behavioural difficulties. The early identification of such speech and language difficulty and prompt intervention are therefore essential. (Section 3:85 *Code of Practice*, 1994.)

Procedures for identification and assessment of pupils with special educational needs are also outlined in the *Code of Practice*: they follow a series of 'stages' and form the basis for identification in all settings even for preschool youngsters.

The role of the Health Authority

District Health Authorities and National Health Service (NHS) Trusts must inform the parents and the appropriate LEA when they form the opinion that a child under the age of five may have special educational needs. They must also inform the parents if they believe that a particular voluntary organisation is likely to be able to give the parents advice or assistance in connection with any special educational needs that the child may have. (Section 332 of the Education (Consolidation) Act 1996.)

The designated medical officer, usually a community paediatrician, is responsible for checking that the District Health Authority has arrangements for ensuring that the Trusts and general practitioners provide child health services. The designated officer must:

- Inform the LEA about children who may have special educational needs
- Provide medical advice for the assessment of the child
- Consider the resources available to children through the Health Service (e.g. access to specific therapy treatments – speech, physiotherapy).

The designated medical officer is also responsible for identifying a named contact for schools (usually the school doctor) to give advice when necessary and co-ordinate the provision made by the Health Service for the child when a variety of 'fund holders' are responsible for the purchasing of services.

The 'stages' of identifying, assessing and making provision for children with special educational needs involve access to a range of specialists and services. At the preschool level many concerns can be addressed very quickly with advice perhaps from the health visitor. Some children are identified virtually from birth as being youngsters who will require a significant amount of support.

However, regardless of the level of difficulty, early identification ensures the best possible outcome for the child.

The green paper (October 1997) *Excellence for All Children,* presented by the Secretary of State for Education and Employment, David Blunkett, highlights the need for early identification of learning difficulties:

The best way to tackle educational disadvantage is to get in early. When educational failure becomes entrenched, pupils can move from demoralisation to disruptive behaviour and truancy. Early diagnosis and appropriate intervention improves the prospects of children with special educational needs, and reduces the need for expensive intervention later on. For some children, giving more effective attention to early signs of difficulty can prevent the development of special educational needs… An integrated approach by child health professionals, social services and education staff is needed right from the start, making full use of the children's services planning process. (DfEE 1997)

The stages in the identification and assessment of preschool children are shown in Figure 7.1. Initially parents may discuss their concerns with the health visitor or GP who may then refer directly to the Child Development Team or other external specialists. If there are problems with feeding or toilet training, advice from the health visitor and a structure for developing the necessary skills may be sufficient so the child does not progress beyond Stages 1 or 2. The child may have some difficulties with language development and the involvement of a speech therapist at Stage 3 may provide the child and parent with the necessary materials and activities to overcome the problem. If the child's needs are deemed to be more complex, a multidisciplinary assessment by the Child Development Team may provide sufficient information for the Local Education Authority to move towards statutory assessment.

In many areas the 'provision' for preschool children is available when the 'need' is identified without the requirement of having to proceed to statutory assessment. This would include home-based teaching services such as Portage and support from therapists in speech and occupational/physiotherapy. Early intervention can be extremely effective: many youngsters enter the nursery and reception class no longer identified as having special educational needs.

Many preschool youngsters identified as dyspraxic, usually referred via a speech therapist, with appropriate intervention can achieve educationally as well as their peers by the end of Key Stage 1. Currently in Durham the vast majority of the children identified with dyspraxia access resourcing at Stage 3: more than 80 per cent of these pupils never progress beyond this to Stage 4.

Where children are not identified as having special educational needs before they reach statutory school age it is usually the class teacher who has concerns about the progress a child is making. Figure 7.2 outlines the procedures for identification and assessment.

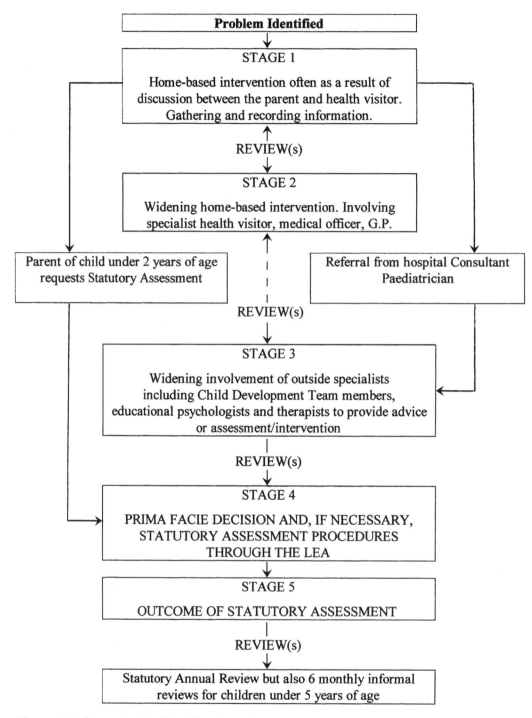

Figure 7.1 Stages in the identification and assessment of preschool children

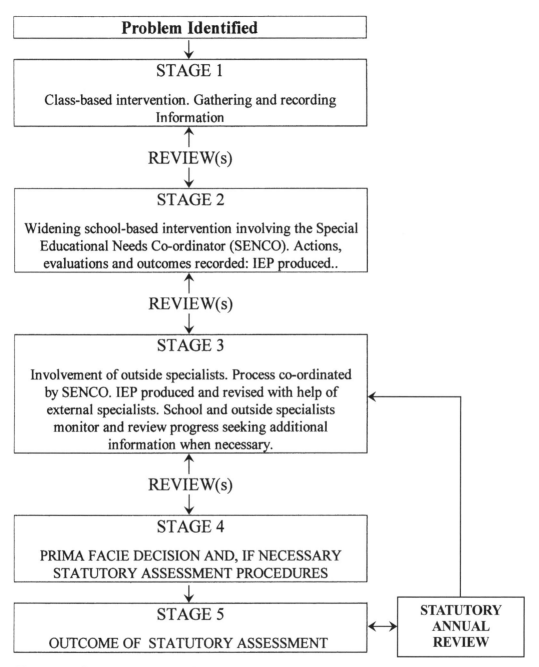

Figure 7.2 Stages in the identification and assessment of school age pupils

Obtaining a diagnosis of dyspraxia

The route of the referral can affect the 'diagnosis'. As discussed in the first chapter, there are many behaviours associated with more than one developmental disorder. Poor concentration and an inability to remain on task are common features in most. Language difficulties, certainly delayed onset of speech, are evident in many cases of dyslexia, dyspraxia and autistic spectrum disorders. Problems with co-ordination can be observed in a child with generalised learning difficulties, specific learning difficulties or without any learning difficulties at all! Assessment should not focus on one area of development because if a particular condition is sought the 'symptoms' will be found.

Parents often say, 'I want my child to be assessed for dyslexia' or 'I've seen a checklist for dyspraxia and I ticked 7 out of the 10 boxes. It describes my child: do you think I should get a diagnosis?' Professionals must be open-minded throughout their involvement with the child or adult and not at the outset assess for a specific condition. A diagnosis should be given only when sufficient information is available to do so. This includes:

- Whenever possible, a detailed developmental history which includes information about factors before and after birth
- Parents' impressions about the presenting difficulties
- A report from a member of the school staff who can give information about attainments
- Information about the child's general health: is there any evidence of allergy; is there a family history of any developmental disorder?
- When appropriate, a neuropsychological profile: this will assist in obtaining a differential diagnosis, particularly when other conditions are occurring comorbidly
- An assessment of perceptual and motor skills: a comparison can then be made with attainment and cognitive function to determine whether there are significant discrepancies
- Additional information from anyone else involved, e.g. speech therapist, optometrist, to provide a comprehensive picture of skill development in all areas.

How can a diagnosis help?

A diagnosis alleviates a great deal of stress in parents who have known that there is something different about their child but have not been able to identify exactly what it is. The child realises that he/she does not carry the responsibility for being poor at maths or being unable to follow a series of instructions. A diagnosis will allow for the appropriate differentiation of curricular material to ensure its accessibility. Visual clues can supplement class discussion. Teachers can consider ways to overcome recording difficulties when the child is required to commit anything to paper. It will be recognised that the child is not being deliberately disruptive or aggressive towards his peers. Structured sessions involving other members of the peer group to improve social skills are extremely beneficial.

A diagnosis can be the 'key' to additional resources if funding for provision depends on identification of a special educational need and the subsequent issue of a Statement.

'Systems' are in place to identify and assess youngsters with dyspraxia and this may be undertaken entirely by the school or with reference to outside specialists. Their effectiveness varies greatly between different Local Education and Health Authorities. Preschool children possibly have the best opportunity for multidisciplinary assessment because Child Development Teams are established in most areas. The success of this system depends largely on the health visitor and GP being aware of the aspects of child development in early years which are symptomatic of developmental dyspraxia.

Children of school age continue to be able to access multidisciplinary assessment but often there are very long waiting lists (18 months–2 years) to see some specialists.

Adults find it virtually impossible to obtain a referral to the appropriate professional for assessment through the National Health Service. In some areas psychologists working for the Employment Service become involved but such cases are rare: this is an issue that needs to be addressed as a matter of urgency.

It is essential that adults with dyspraxia have access to careers guidance as such a high proportion have failed to secure work of a permanent nature (Portwood 1999) or indeed any work at all. This is not because of any major difficulty on the part of the employee but because of the unsuitability of the employment recommended. One adult with whom I was involved over a period of six months was placed initially as a waiter in a local restaurant. Not only did he have difficulty remembering the order (he had to remember it because he couldn't write it down sufficiently quickly) but he could not manage to carry a tray full of dishes from the kitchen to the table without accident. After a month he was offered an alternative placement in an office. On arrival he discovered it was a telesales company: needless to say recording telephone conversations by hand was not a strong point either.

Provision for pupils with dyspraxia: mainstream vs special school placement

Children and adults with developmental dyspraxia are placed along a 'continuum' of difficulty. If a 'specialist' placement is sought it is often only possible to support fully the 'primary' presenting difficulty. If the child for example has problems with the articulation of speech, should they transfer to a language unit? If so, what programmes are available to develop motor skills, improve perceptual ability and promote social relationships? If the placement specialises in working with children who have physical difficulties will the curriculum be adapted to address the child's specific learning difficulties in mathematics and subjects such as geography when map reading is required? Perhaps the child would benefit more in an environment where teaching focuses on using multisensory approaches to improve basic skills in numeracy and literacy.

In the end a decision about educational placement has to be determined by:

- Deciding which environment occasions the least stress for the child (if they are unhappy the most focused and appropriate provision available would not achieve the expected improvement)
- What can be done to address all the areas of need identified through assessment
- Which offers the child the best opportunity to feel 'included'.

The 1996 Education Act places on Local Education Authorities a duty to integrate children with special educational needs into mainstream schools although it is acknowledged that some will continue to have their needs met in special schools.

Inclusion and integration do not mean the same thing: integration implies that the child is placed physically within a mainstream environment. McCormick and Shiefelbusch (1997) state:

> Inclusion is not episodic visits to the mainstream classroom for art, music and/or circle time... inclusion is 'belonging'. It is every child (whether 'statemented' or otherwise) having whatever resources and supports he/she needs, and a challenging educational programme that is geared to his/her abilities, needs and interests... It is everyone (children and adults alike) welcoming and valuing abilities as well as disabilities and learning to respect and depend on one another.

Integration, in an environment in which the child does feel included, means that children with special educational needs have the opportunity to be educated with their peer groups. If placement is regarded as being on a continuum from local mainstream classroom at one end to special school or unit at the other, given access to all the necessary support, the mainstream environment would be the preferred option: in many instances parents choose a special school placement purely on the grounds of class size. The child is more confident when he can easily access the teacher and does not feel he is the focus of class attention.

Local Education Authorities are developing policies for inclusion which mean that mainstream schools are making provision to meet the needs of local children regardless of whether they have disabilities or special educational needs. Special schools will remain for the foreseeable future although the majority currently have close links with local mainstream schools. This provides the opportunity for children from either school to be integrated and included in both the mainstream and special school environment.

Requests for special examination arrangements

Youngsters with developmental dyspraxia do not require a Statement to be given special consideration in examinations. Arrangements can be made to support children, not only in external examinations but also with their assessments at Key Stages in primary and secondary education.

Developmental dyspraxia is a specific learning difficulty and generally the child's verbal skills exceed their ability to process and record ideas manually. Special arrangements can be made for pupils completing their Standard Attainment Tests if the school contacts the locally appointed moderator and completes the appropriate paperwork. The class/subject teacher is required to provide 'evidence' of the discrepancies in the child's ability to perform specified tasks. It is not necessary to obtain additional information or refer to an outside specialist for assessment.

Until recently, requests for special arrangements for students taking external examinations were made by educational psychologists. It is now possible for teachers who fulfil the training requirements for the identification of dyslexia to make the request. The information requested is detailed in Figure 7.3.

Data from standardised tests should be provided wherever possible. The student must have a history of specific learning difficulties and attainments in literacy and numeracy must be quoted.

Cognitive assessment data would usually include the individual sub-test scores achieved in the Wechsler Intelligence Scale for Children. Discrepancies between tasks which had a perceptual/motor component or a requirement for auditory sequencing and those which assessed general verbal skills and visual sequencing would be highlighted.

An explanation must be given as to why the student would be severely disadvantaged if he/she does not have access to additional time, a word processor or an amanuensis: i.e. the student's ability to record information does not reflect his/her understanding of the subject.

If the request for special arrangement is agreed it is valid for a two year period after which updated assessment information must be made available to the examination board.

Students with developmental dyspraxia following courses in further and higher education have the same entitlement to special arrangements.

REQUEST FOR SPECIAL EXAMINATION ARRANGEMENTS

PSYCHOLOGICAL ASSESSMENT REPORT

This form should be completed by an appropriately qualified psychologist or an appropriately qualified teacher.

Full names of candidate :

Date of Birth   School/College

Literacy Attainments

Outline the candidate's history of literacy difficulties and any of the following: the results of recent tests of reading accuracy and speed, spelling, writing speed and legibility; names, dates and 'test ceilings' of standardised tests used. Interpret the results in terms of their implications for the examination.

Figure 7.3 Special examination arrangements

Cognitive Assessments

Provide evidence that the candidate can cope with the content of the examination. Give details of assessments, for example, WISC, Raven's Matrices, the date of assessments and the test conclusions or results.

Other Relevant Information

Explain why you think the candidate has learning difficulties severe enough to warrant special examination arrangements.

Figure 7.3 Special examination arrangements (continued)

Detail any other information to be taken into account, such as normal methods of working e.g. The use of word processor, special arrangements that have been allowed in other examinations (for example, Key Stage 3), perceptual, attentional or co-ordination difficulties and any relevant emotional factors.

Is any additional psychological information enclosed with this form?   YES/NO

_____

Name of author of this report -

Are You:

A Chartered Educational Psychologist?   YES/NO

A Full/Affiliate member of the Association of Educational Psychologists?   YES/NO

Employed as an Educational Psychologist by a LEA   YES/NO

Other ....

I certify that the above information is accurate and that all assessments were carried out by a psychologist or appropriately qualified person.

Signed: .... Date ....

Figure 7.3 Special examination arrangements (continued)

Chapter 8

Optimising the educational environment

Preschool educational experience has a greater influence on the development of perceptual skills, spatial awareness and motor skills than the development of language. This, as discussed in Chapter 3, is the result of predominantly right hemispheric function that is evident in children until the age of four.

Educators involved with preschool children have increasing concerns about the number of youngsters entering nursery/playgroups already showing signs of significant motor and perceptual difficulties that are at variance with skill development in other areas. Preschool providers, therefore, offer children the optimum environment to improve their developing skills if this environment is structured both indoors and outdoors with a variety of play activities. Wetton (1997) has undertaken extensive assessment of the development of motor skills in young children and identified a small percentage of preschool children who are capable of performing complex gross-motor movements expected of an eight year old. However, she states that in the same sample virtually none of the children could demonstrate the finer-motor skills (eye – hand co-ordination) evident in pupils aged six. This confirms that these developments depend on a level of neurological maturity and can only be enhanced with access to a structured programme of intervention: preschool children do not acquire them in a free-choice play situation. Where such difficulties have been identified, preschool children will benefit from structured play and some teacher-directed activities.

There are many reasons why a proportion of children enter preschool and nursery with delays in some areas of development. They have had a variety of early experiences: some enabled to run and climb outdoors while others have been restricted by their home environment, e.g. in flats or living in the centre of town where traffic restricts freedom to play. Many youngsters will have selected interactive computer games or videos as an alternative to outdoor experiences.

If educators do decide to offer a structured learning programme to improve the perceptual and motor skills of preschool children about whom they have concerns, it is important to understand what level the children can be expected to achieve, given their age: what is the accepted 'norm' for neurological competence?

It is difficult to talk in terms of the percentage of children expected to be identified with significant delays in the development of motor skills. It is expected that analysis of the entire population of preschool children would produce a 'normal' distribution curve of ability; what is a cause for concern is that young children are generally afforded fewer opportunities to develop their motor skills and teachers report a higher proportion of children about whom they have concerns. It is insufficient, therefore, to say that only pupils whose abilities are below the 2nd percentile (when considering the whole population in that age range) should be considered for intervention. It may well be that as many as 20 per cent or 30 per cent of the pupils are not achieving at the level expected for their age and maturity.

To identify the children who can benefit from intervention it is important to have an understanding of the expected motor patterns present in youngsters who are three years old and not use selection procedures that are based entirely on percentile scores.

A summary of expected attainments for children entering preschool provision at the age of three is given below.

1. *Gross motor skills*

Children at three should be able to:
• Crawl through a tunnel co-ordinating arms and legs appropriately
• Walk competently backwards and forwards
• Walk sideways
• Run competently
• Walk on tiptoes
• Jump on the spot or from a low step, feet together
• Climb up and down stairs placing one foot on each step
• Walk heel/toe along a measured distance of 3 metres
• Balance along a plank, slightly raised (10cm) from the floor
• Balance on either foot for 5+ seconds.

2. *Co-ordination skills*
• Kick a ball with each foot
• Throw a small ball with each hand
• Pedal a tricycle and change direction appropriately
• Catch a large ball thrown from a distance of 3m with two hands.

3. *Fine motor and perceptual skills*
• Show hand preference
• Replace small pegs in board
• Build towers of 6+ bricks (2.5cm in size)
• Reassemble screw toys/replace bottle tops
• Thread a sequence of large beads
• Complete a 6-piece inset puzzle, jigsaw
• Hold writing implement (crayon/pencil) and make marks on paper
• Copy simple shapes (Figures 8.1 and 8.2).

The child is asked to copy the lines and shapes after teacher demonstration. The proformas provide a record of attainment and can be practised both in the educational and home environment.

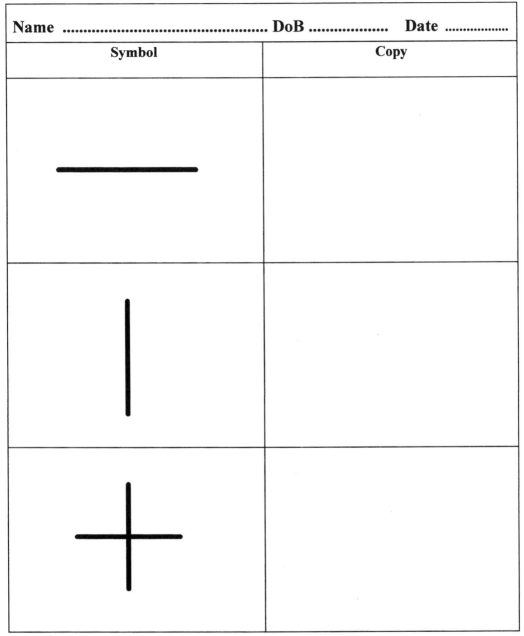

Name .... DoB .... Date	
Symbol	**Copy**

Figure 8.1 Assessment of fine motor/perceptual skills (A)

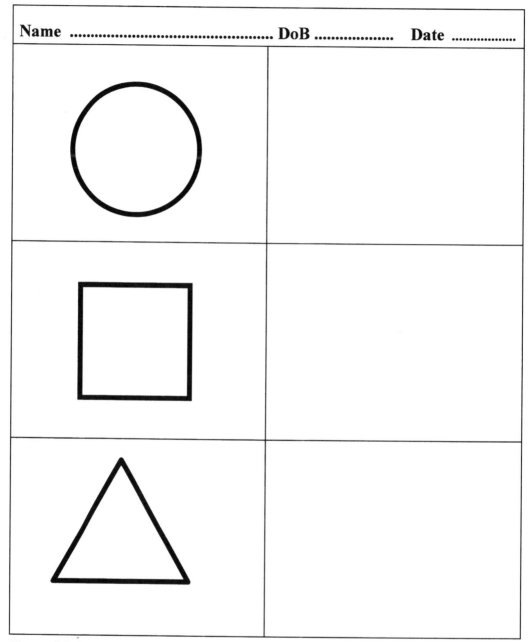

Figure 8.2 Assessment of fine motor/perceptual skills (B)

Some children will not have developed the skills necessary to complete these tasks because they have had insufficient experience; nevertheless such youngsters should be identified for low level structured intervention. Adult involvement has a direct effect on the preschool child's choice of activity. Specifically targeted activities can improve the child's skills without access to which their development would be left to chance. Wetton (1997) says: 'We can no longer leave this learning to the osmosis approach in which children select their own play and as a consequence their own learning activities.'

Intervention

Children do not like to be identified as different from others in their peer group and in an inclusive environment, wherever possible, provision should be made for pupils with learning difficulties or any other disability without removing them to work in isolation from the rest of the group. Ideally, where there are motor difficulties the needs of these youngsters should be addressed through an exercise programme that targets specific areas of competence but in which the whole class can participate.

The Youth Sport Trust in association with the Sports Council, the British Association of Advisers and Lecturers in Physical Education and the Physical Education Association (UK) has produced a series of progressive programmes to give children the opportunity to develop a range of physical skills. The ideas presented are designed for the inclusion of all children.

The programmes are:

Top Tots: The first in the series: its aim is to introduce simple games at home to children aged 18 months to 3 years.

It is acknowledged that children of this age play independently and alongside each other rather than cooperatively. An adult helper directs the activities of individuals and small groups of youngsters. The activities are organised into four groups and can be altered to reflect the child's experience and ability.

- Aiming games
- Running and taking games
- Batting games
- Collecting-on-the-move games.

Top Start: Provides activities to encourage the physical development of children aged 3–5 years; it develops basic movement and ball skills and is ideal for the nursery and preschool environment.

The scheme identifies four essential areas that are highlighted in the 'Desirable Outcomes for Physical Development'

- Basic motor skills
- Moving around in different ways (mobility)
- Spatial awareness
  - knowing where you are and the shapes your body can make.
- Co-ordination and control
  - physical control and balance.

- Aiming/predicting/estimating
  - using small equipment to roll, throw and aim.

Top Play: This has been designed to be implemented by teachers to support PE programmes for 4–9 year olds in primary school.

The core skills identified are:

- Rolling a ball
- Receiving a ball
- Running, jumping, hopping
- Travelling with a ball
- Throwing and catching
- Striking
- Kicking.

Top Sport: This final programme is designed to introduce specific sports to 7–11 year olds in primary school.

Each programme is supported by a resource pack and equipment is available from Davies The Sports People. Local Education Authorities have identified registered trainers who advise on the appropriate use of materials and delivery of the programmes.

Some children cannot have all their needs met in the school or home environment and attend clinics where they have access to movement specialists – physio/occupational therapists – who will offer individual programmes and provide additional equipment when necessary. However, resources are limited and the majority of children with delayed motor development and difficulties with spatial perceptual skills depend on identification and school-based intervention.

When children reach statutory school age it is important that information about their development is made available from the preschool provider. This can be from a variety of sources including specific activity schemes such as Tumble Tots who complete a record of achievement for youngsters during the final term prior to school transfer.

In September 1998 the Government introduced the 'Baseline Assessment' of pupils that should be completed within seven weeks of the child's start in primary school. Many Local Education Authorities produced their own 'Schemes' which were then submitted for endorsement by the Qualification and Curriculum Authority. The information from this 'Baseline Assessment' can be invaluable if it is used from an early stage to identify children 'at risk' of school failure. For the majority of these youngsters low level intervention in the reception class improves their skills to such an extent that at the end of Key Stage 1 they are achieving at the expected level for their age. Preschool data provides insight into the child's experiences and facilitates more accurate interpretation of the information from the Baseline Assessment.

The majority of the schemes consider:

- Language and literacy
  - reading
  - writing
  - speaking and listening

- Mathematics
  - using and applying numbers
- Personal and social development
  - relationships
  - independence
- Physical development
- Creative development
- Knowledge and understanding of the world.

Where the comorbidity of developmental disorders is high, as is the case for children aged four, it is unnecessary to 'label' the child as having dyspraxia or dyslexia if provision is available to develop the necessary skills, especially when many of these youngsters would be achieving their expected targets before the age of seven.

To use the 'Baseline' data effectively it is necessary to compare the results of pupils of the same age and sex. If the developmental differences between boys and girls are not taken into account whole cohorts of 'failing' boys will be identified. The Durham scheme for Baseline Assessment, 'Flying Start', was piloted in a number of Local Authorities before its introduction in 1998. Analysis of the results of more than 7,000 pupils highlighted major sex differences. Of children scoring above the 50th percentile, when all areas of development were considered, two-thirds were girls whereas below the 50th percentile two-thirds were boys. The same results have been reflected nationally. This is not because boys are in any way disadvantaged in the preschool environment: it is that girls are more mature at the age of four in the areas of development that were measured.

Reception class teachers were questioned as to the most common areas of difficulty experienced by youngsters transferring from nursery education into a more structured environment. Some youngsters had not had the benefits of any preschool education.

Responses highlighted the increasing incidence of behavioural problems and youngsters who were unable to remain on task for periods in excess of five minutes. Many teachers were concerned that youngsters were entering reception class with significant communication difficulties and they stated that this in itself had a profound effect on their behaviour. In addition, they had concerns about a small group of youngsters who struggled to develop basic skills in reading and writing, and to acquire a conceptual understanding of number. Attention was drawn to those youngsters who had limited perceptual ability with additional problems co-ordinating fine and gross motor movement.

To identify children who have 'specific' rather than generalised learning difficulties it is necessary to consider discrepancies in attainments. I completed my own analysis of the results achieved by pupils in the Durham Assessment and followed their progress over a three year period. It became evident that there were descriptors in the 'Baseline' that could identify pupils aged four who without intervention were diagnosed as dyspraxic by the age of seven. Generally, comprehension was significantly better than expressive language and ability to convey information by pictures or writing. Motor and perceptual skills were also depressed in relation to other scores.

Case study 1: Thomas

Thomas was a youngster who through classroom observation and Baseline Assessment was identified within the first term following transfer to reception class as a child who was competent in many areas of development but had specific problems with drawing, copying, understanding number, creativity and co-ordination. He had been asked to reproduce the shapes of Figures 8.1, 8.2 and 8.3 but could manage only the horizontal/vertical lines and the circle.

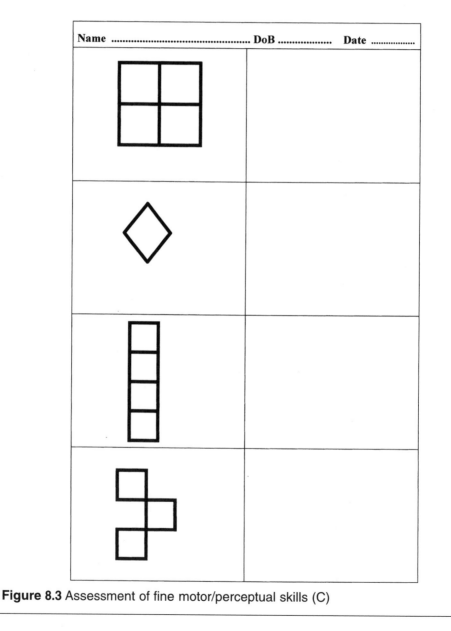

Figure 8.3 Assessment of fine motor/perceptual skills (C)

Thomas's Baseline profile (chronological age 4 years 8 months):

- Language and literacy 11/24   45.8
- Mathematics...2/16   12.5
- Personal and social development............................10/16   62.5
- Physical development..1/ 8   12.5
- Creative development...1/ 8   12.5
- Knowledge and understanding 5/ 8   62.5

Average   34.7

There were different totals for the descriptors in each section so the scores are expressed as percentages to enable comparisons to be made between attainments before and after intervention.

Thomas was provided with a variety of activities designed to improve perceptual skills. They included access to 'Write from the Start' by Teodorescu/Addy and a series of prepared templates: Figures 8.4, 8.5 and 8.6. Thomas was given a selection of black and white squares and asked to reproduce the pattern. Even with teacher demonstration he struggled for two weeks with Figure 8.4: by the end of the first month he had mastered them all and became competent in producing more complex designs, Figure 8.7.

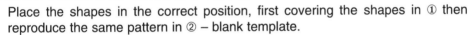

Place the shapes in the correct position, first covering the shapes in ① then reproduce the same pattern in ② – blank template.

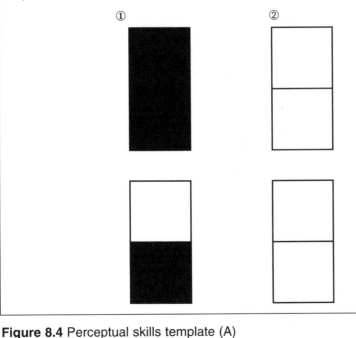

Figure 8.4 Perceptual skills template (A)

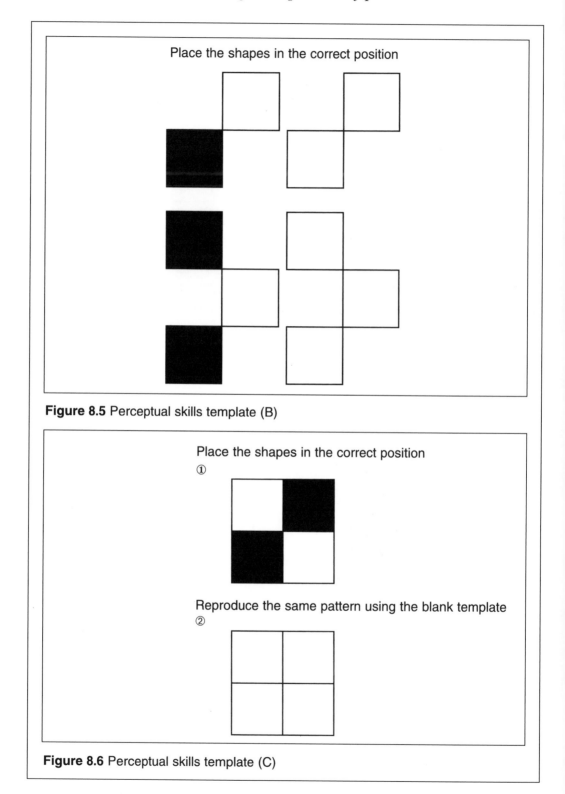

Figure 8.5 Perceptual skills template (B)

Figure 8.6 Perceptual skills template (C)

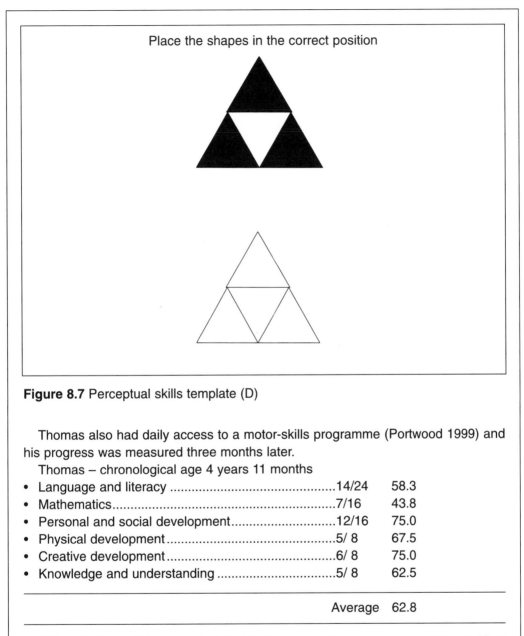

Figure 8.7 Perceptual skills template (D)

Thomas also had daily access to a motor-skills programme (Portwood 1999) and his progress was measured three months later.

Thomas – chronological age 4 years 11 months

- Language and literacy 14/24   58.3
- Mathematics..7/16   43.8
- Personal and social development.............................12/16   75.0
- Physical development...5/ 8   67.5
- Creative development...6/ 8   75.0
- Knowledge and understanding 5/ 8   62.5

| | Average | 62.8 |

Although it would be expected that in three months progress would be evident without any specified intervention, when a comparison is made between the percentage increases in the six areas assessed, far greater improvement is observed where programmes of intervention have been targeted.

Case study 2: Jack

Older pupils have benefited from similar programmes of intervention. Jack was seven when he was identified as having developmental dyspraxia. His co-ordination was poor and he found it impossible to produce recognisable pictures (Figure 8.8). Jack's handwriting was illegible: he struggled even to copy underneath prepared material provided by his teacher (Figure 8.9).

Figure 8.8 Jack, aged seven: free drawing

Figure 8.9 Jack, aged seven: handwriting sample

Jack was keen to develop his skills and any activities completed during the day were practised at home in the evening. They included prepared sheets from the Frostig programme and balancing exercises on his skateboard. After 12 months following a prescribed developmental programme he asked whether he could be shown how to skip. This was a child who on initial assessment was unable to turn a rope, tied at one end, through more than two revolutions before the movement pattern broke down. Jack's determination to master this skill was evident: his parents were aware of 'thudding noises' coming from his bedroom late into the night. Two weeks later Jack was triumphant. He had not allowed anyone to observe him 'training' but the end result enabled him to challenge every other pupil in the class in terms of speed of rope-turning and number of successful 'skips'.

Jack's success in skipping coincided with the inter-school sports competition. He won the three-legged, egg and spoon and sack races! Jack no longer displayed the classical signs of poor co-ordination expected in a youngster with developmental dyspraxia. In addition, his handwriting improved dramatically (Figure 8.10) and four terms after his 'diagnosis' he was completely integrated in his class without requiring access to additional support.

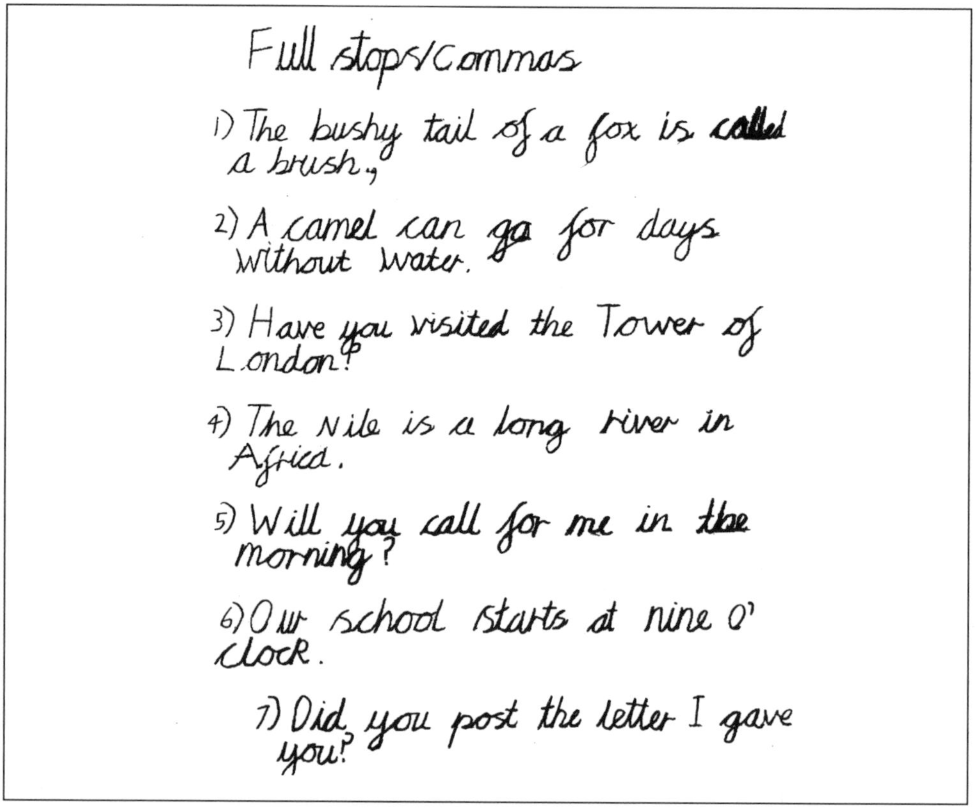

Full stops/commas

1) The bushy tail of a fox is called a brush.,

2) A camel can go for days without water.

3) Have you visited the Tower of London?

4) The Nile is a long river in Africa.

5) Will you call for me in the morning?

6) Our school starts at nine o' clock.

7) Did you post the letter I gave you?

Figure 8.10 Jack, aged nine: handwriting sample

Case study 3: Peter

Peter, aged ten, had struggled with class work, particularly when there was a requirement to record information manually. He was becoming more disaffected with school and very reluctant to attend. He complained constantly about headaches and stomach pains particularly on days when PE was timetabled.

Peter was very articulate and couldn't understand why some children whom he felt to be less able than himself could produce well-formed handwriting in the allotted time. Homework that should have been finished in half an hour sometimes took all evening; then there was the additional unfinished class work that had been brought home for completion.

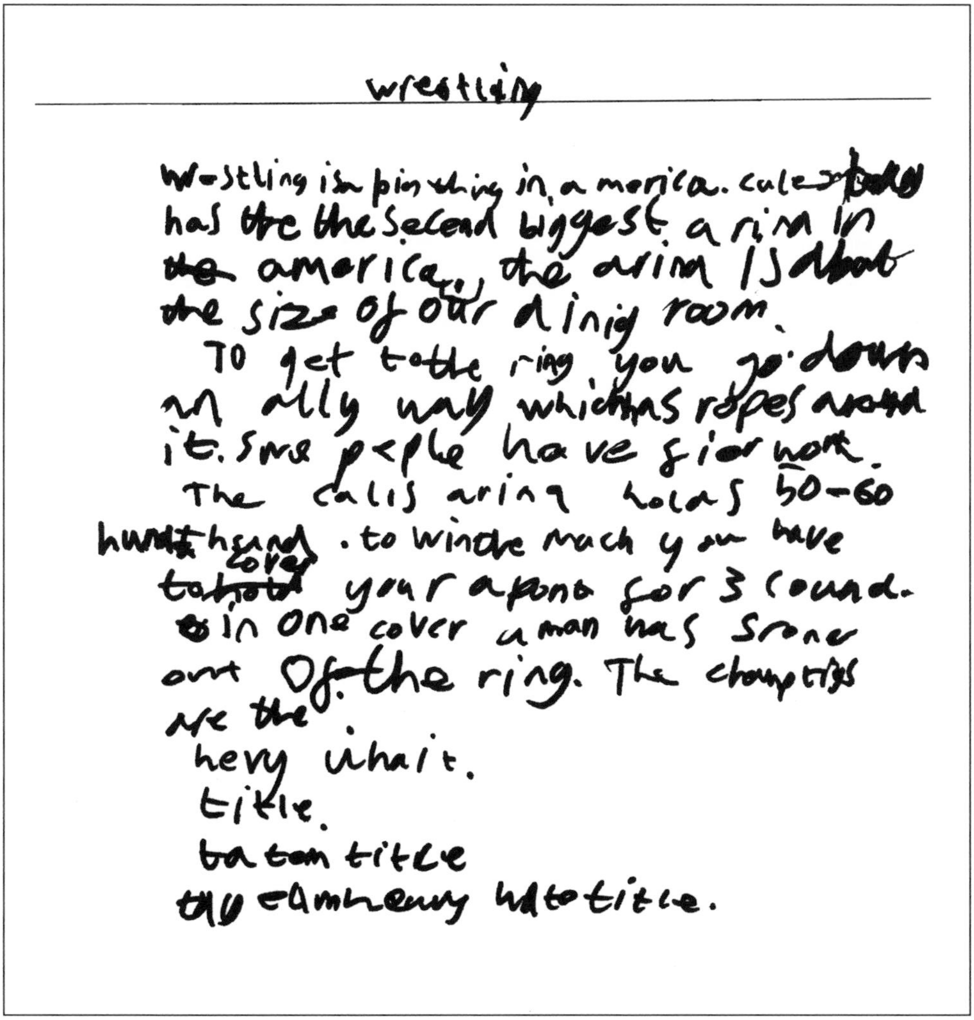

wrestling

Westling is pinshing in a merica. cale
has the the Second biggest a rim in
the america, the arina is about
the size of our dinig room.
TO get to the ring you go down
an ally way which has ropes arond
it. Sme peple have fior work.
The calis aring holas 50-60
hunthend. to winthe mach you have
cover your apono for 3 round.
in one cover a man has srone
out Of the ring. The chomptigs
are the
hevy whait.
title.
ba tam title
the camhenry hateo title.

Figure 8.11 Peter, aged ten: handwriting sample

Youngsters with dyspraxia should not be expected to spend often as much as eight times longer completing a piece of work than their peers. Material should be differentiated to reduce the need for lengthy hand-written responses. The pupils' understanding of the subject could be assessed orally or perhaps through multiple choice questions. It took Peter about an hour to produce the work shown in Figure 8.11; even then, after all his effort, it was still unreadable.

Peter followed a motor skills programme which was predominantly home-based. It can be difficult for parents who are working with their own children, particularly if activities are organised in the evening after a full day in school. Nevertheless, Peter was another youngster who was committed to helping himself: after two terms not only was there a noticeable improvement in school work, but Peter had become more positive about himself and was beginning to enjoy school. Staff were also seeing the change and encouraged him to continue his efforts.

Peter still thinks it takes 'forever' to finish a page of handwriting but at least the result (Figure 8.12) is now accessible to those other than Peter. He continues to work on a daily programme and he is following a course of perceptual training.

For youngsters of primary school age there are national assessments of basic skills at the end of Key Stage 1 (6–7 years) and Key Stage 2 (10–11 years). Attainments in language and literacy are measured by assessing spelling and handwriting as well as reading and comprehension. It is important that teachers base their opinions about the child not on presentation of material, but on content.

My French Holiday

This year we went to France. We stayed in the Loir valley, my freind was there at the same time.
We had been there before, this year we went at the time of the eclipse.

The we went to paris and Euro disney.

Figure 8.12 Peter: handwriting sample two terms after intervention

---

Case study 4: Jonathan

Jonathan was six years old and preparing for his Key Stage 1 SATs (Standard Attainment Tests). Although he presented as a bright, articulate child, interpreting his written work was at best very time-consuming. Shortly after Christmas, he was observed gazing through the classroom window, talking to himself about the patterns the snow made as it fell. After a while he requested a pencil and began to write. First, he divided the page into four horizontal strips then marked them off using five vertical lines – making six boxes on each strip (24 in total). He then wrote furiously. After 20 minutes he presented his work. (Figure 8.13, word processed in Figure 8.14)

Jonathan saw the difficulty his teacher had deciphering the letter shapes and words which had been spelt phonetically. He took the sheet and began to read. As he spoke, she realised that the sectioned off page represented four verses each of six lines. The child's understanding of nature and his creative ability became more evident as he moved through the verses. How easy it would have been to have missed the content of the poem and identified the child perhaps as being a low-achiever, as might have been the case on spelling and presentation alone.

Children and adults with dyspraxia have great difficulty organising their thoughts. Jonathan, by splitting up the page, was able to provide his own structure. Teachers can improve the learning abilities of dyspraxic pupils if they provide them with a structure and present information in a tangible and highly visual way. Dyspraxic pupils do not have particular difficulty understanding the information given to them: the problem is recording and remembering it.

An effective system of 'note' taking that utilises visual memory has been developed by Buzan (1997). He identified a number of factors which facilitated improved recall of information:
- Selection of key words
- Formation of images
- Organisation, i.e. provide structure for ideas and identify associations between them.

Russel (1997) states that the brain imposes its own organisation on the information it stores and the mechanisms of organising the material are in themselves helpful to memory. The term used by Buzan to describe his system of recalling is 'Mind Mapping'. He suggests that a key word describing the topic is placed in the centre of the page: this should be linked to a strong visual image. This well-defined centre then has a number of sub-centres radiating from it. As images are more easily recalled than words, the mind map becomes increasingly effective as more visual representations are included. The following points should be considered.
- Key words are more visual when printed than when written in script
- Coloured images are more easily remembered than black and white
- Three-dimensional shapes provide the map with a more defined visual structure
- Where possible, include pictures in the structure
- Make associations using arrows.

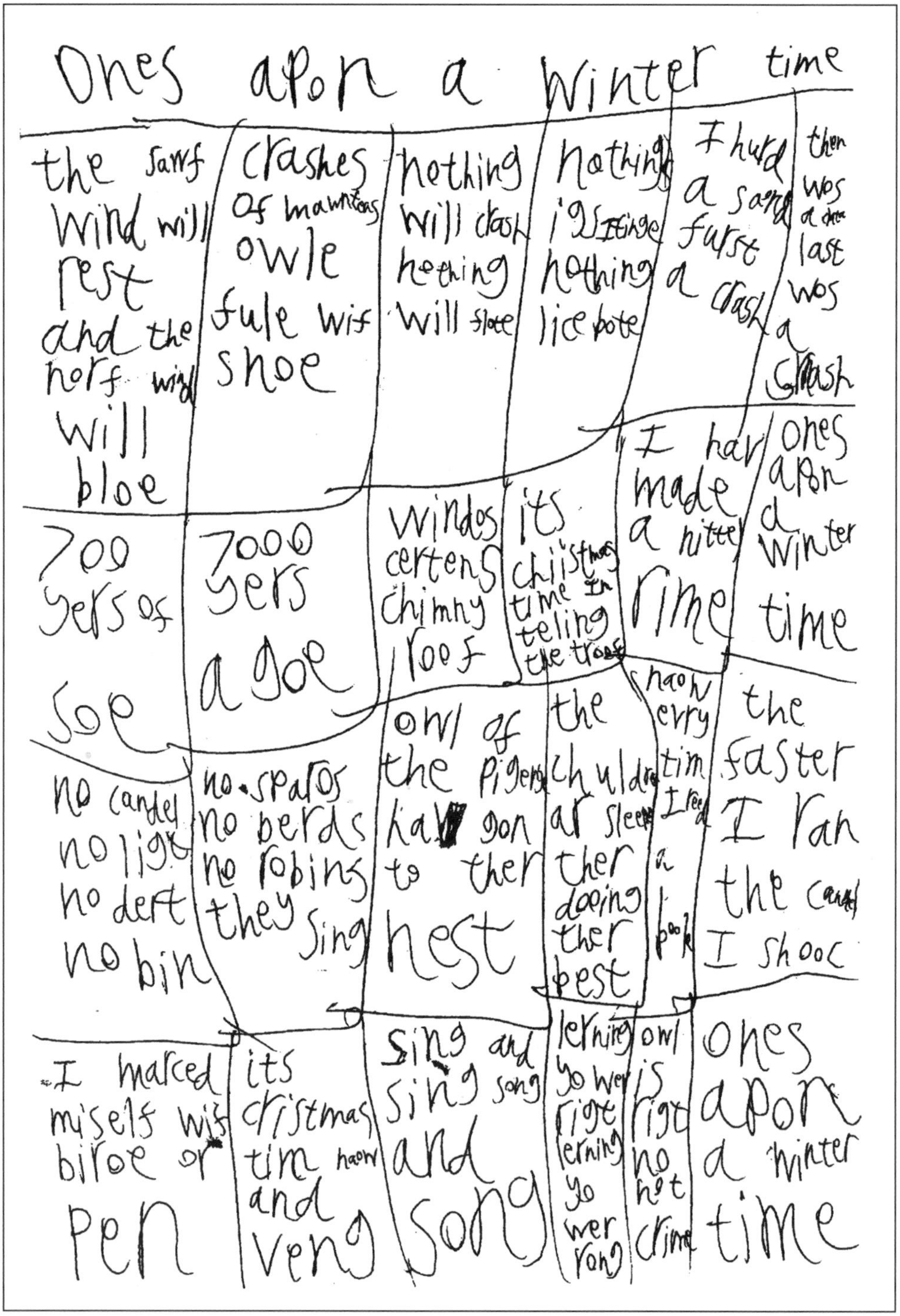

Figure 8.13 Jonathan, aged six: 'Once upon a winter time', handwritten

Once Upon a Winter's Time -- Jonathan (aged 6)

The South wind will rest and the North wind will blow,
Crashes of mountains all full with snow.
Nothing will crash, nothing will float
Nothing's exciting, nothing like boat.
I heard a sound first a crash
Then was a clatter, last was a smash.

Seven hundred years or so,
Seven thousand years ago,
Windows, curtains, chimney, roof
It's Christmas time - I'm telling the truth.
I have made a little rhyme
Once upon a winter time.

No candle, no light, no dirt, no bin
No sparrows, no birds, no robins they sing.
All of the pigeons have gone to their nest
The children are sleeping - they're doing their best.
Now every time I read a book
The faster I ran, the candle I shook

I marked myself with biro or pen
It's Christmas time now and then
Sing and Sing, Song and song
Learning you were right, learning you were wrong.
All is right no not crime
Once upon a winter time.

Figure 8.14 Jonathan, aged six: 'Once upon a winter time', word processed

The responsibility for producing the mind map should not always rest with the child. The teacher may choose to present subject information to the class in the same way. Recently I observed a primary school teacher discussing the Fire of London with a group of seven year olds (Figure 8. 15).

The teacher began with a box of flames in the centre and then moved outwards identifying the people and places which were key features of the event. The children were encouraged to 'record' discussion through a series of drawings.

One of the main advantages of mind maps is that by constructing them, the ideas become 'fixed' and can easily be recalled mentally without having to refer back to the 'printed' record. Presentations which are highly visual benefit many more than just those youngsters with developmental dyspraxia. It is important not to be too prescriptive about teaching methods, as personal style must be considered. Children benefit from a variety of approaches and some which have proved successful when used with dyspraxic youngsters have been discussed.

For a variety of reasons some children with dyspraxia do not make the expected progress in the mainstream environment and are placed in a special school or unit. The next chapter examines identification and provision made for youngsters with dyspraxia in a residential school in Durham.

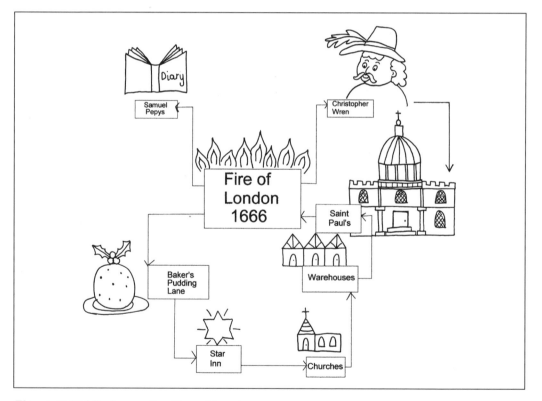

Figure 8.15 Mind map: the Fire of London

Chapter 9

Intervention in a residential setting: Elemore Hall School

Elemore Hall is a school for secondary age pupils and caters for boys and girls. All pupils admitted to the school have a statement of special educational needs and are referred with emotional, behavioural and learning difficulties. The nature of these difficulties has been sufficient to seriously hinder their progress in mainstream or other special schools. Many of the youngsters also experience difficulties in the environment outside school and to meet the needs of these youngsters Elemore Hall provides specialist education, residential care and therapeutic intervention.

The school is based in a former country house dating back to the 1700s. It is situated in a rural location several miles from Durham City. It has been a school since 1958 and the grounds extend to approximately 30 acres comprising woodland, playing fields and farm land.

The youngsters are supported in school by teachers, child care staff, learning support staff and a range of domestic and ancillary staff. Other agencies, health, social services and support teams from the Education Department are also involved where appropriate.

The staff are highly committed to supporting pupils in their care and during the past two years have identified aspects of training which would be relevant to improving their professional skills. They offer strategies for intervention to address the educational, emotional and social needs of the pupils.

In many educational establishments staff have increasing concerns regarding the number of youngsters who present with symptoms of developmental disorders. Mike Davey, the head teacher at Elemore, prioritised the need, in consultation with staff members, for a raised awareness of the presenting problems of these youngsters. Training needs were addressed as part of a planned programme of professional development where the aim was not only to identify these youngsters but also to offer appropriate intervention.

Mike Davey was aware that a great deal of work was being undertaken in other schools in Durham in relation to pupils with developmental dyspraxia and he believed that a residential school could provide the ideal environment for appropriate intervention. After a detailed discussion between myself, the head teacher and the school psychologist, Lynn Gibson, the methods of identification and intervention were determined.

The teachers, child care and learning support staff attended sessions which considered the neurological principles underlying dyspraxia and presenting behaviours observed in secondary age pupils. Many youngsters were identified during training as likely to benefit from intervention. The staff were committed to providing the necessary support to pupils involved in the programme and the enthusiasm of two key co-ordinators, Barbara Barron and Joan Huntingdon, was overwhelming.

Selection of sample

School staff, after consultation with the school psychologist, were to identify groups of pupils who:

- Presented symptoms of dyspraxia
- Presented symptoms of dyspraxia with other comorbid conditions e.g. dyslexia, Attention Deficit and Hyperactivity Disorder and autistic spectrum disorders
- Presented as having generalised moderate learning difficulties.

It was envisaged that all pupils would follow the same programme of intervention and that this would offer the opportunity to compare the progress of youngsters in each group.

After staff training it was agreed that youngsters who appeared to fulfil the criteria for referral should be assessed as follows:

- Psychometric assessment – the Wechsler Intelligence Scale for Children III UK was used to provide detailed information as to the cognitive profile of all pupils referred.
- Assessment of motor skills (described in Chapter 6).
- Reading and spelling skills assessed using the Wechsler Objective Reading Dimensions test.
- Numeracy skills assessed using standard attainment tests by staff involved.
- Samples of free handwriting to be collected before, during and after intervention.
- Any additional information e.g. assessment by other professionals such as a speech therapist, physiotherapist, child and adolescent psychiatrist.

When the information on each child was made available, 15 pupils from years 7 to 9 were identified. The sample comprised: 13 boys and 2 girls. Ages ranged from 11 years 2 months to 13 years 7 months.

Procedures following pupil identification

- Baseline Motor Assessment (see Figure 9.1)
- Information from initial assessment record
- Sample of 'free' handwriting
- Assessment of time on task prior to intervention measured.

Pupils and their parents gave permission to record the motor assessment. This gave the involved members of staff the opportunity to observe in detail the co-ordination difficulties the youngsters experienced. It also allowed the pupils to observe for themselves their improvement after intervention.

Intervention

It was agreed that youngsters involved in the project would have daily access to a 15/20 minute motor skills programme supervised by a member of staff. Some pupils worked with their peers, others individually. Activities were selected from the *Developmental Dyspraxia* manual (Portwood 1999) which targeted:
• Fine and gross motor co-ordination
• Balance
• Auditory sequencing
• Spatial/perceptual skills.

Monitoring

The programmes were followed from October 1998 until July 1999. Some pupils were given immediate access and others started in January 1999. This was due to staff changes, not project design. Record keeping was essential, not only to monitor progress but also to determine the access of each child to the programme. This included:
• Weekly records of attendance and progress following a motor skills programme
• Assessment of progress on worksheets to develop spatial/perceptual skills
• Collection of samples of handwriting on a monthly basis
• Notes of any significant behavioural changes
• Video recording before, during and after intervention.

The attendance records showed some variance between individuals. Some pupils had been absent for prolonged periods because of illness. A few, owing to the nature of their emotional/behavioural difficulties, had on occasion absconded.

The progress of pupils who had achieved 66 per cent or greater attendance was followed. This involved 11 pupils from the original sample of 15. Ten achieved attendance of 80 per cent or higher.

There were some constraints on the delivery of the programme because of the availability of space. The majority of youngsters used either their living accommodation or a classroom. In the future it is hoped that a local sports hall might be made available.

Post intervention

This involved interviewing each pupil individually and collating information from participating members of staff, i.e. those delivering and monitoring the programme of intervention and the subject teachers and care staff involved at a personal level with the pupils.

In addition, the following areas were reassessed:
• Motor skills
• Reading
• Spelling

- Handwriting
- Numeracy
- Behaviour.

(The proforma to assess baseline motor skills is included, see Figure 9.1.)

Assessment of motor skills

Name ....

Date ....

Record of Information (Personal impressions of programme)
Pupil :

Tutor :

Parallel Lines	
• Tiptoes	
• Heels	
• Heel toe	
• Sides	
Using Single Line	
• Jumping - feet together	
• Crawling	
• Skipping	
• Running	
• Walking	
• Hopping - Right Foot	
- Left Foot	
• Balance - Right Foot	
- Left Foot	
• Finger Sequencing - Right Hand	
- Left Hand	

Figure 9.1 Assessment of motor skills – proforma

Results

It was difficult at the outset to envisage the commitment not only of the staff involved in the project but also of the pupils who were selected for the programme of intervention. The children themselves were thrilled to be selected and did not perceive it in any way as a stigma. The youngsters were keen to attend their daily sessions and other members of their peer group asked whether they could join.

The youngsters could see significant improvements in their attainments and also their social relationships. They were able to build close relationships with the staff members involved and at the end of the project were very anxious that it should continue into the following academic year.

Individual teacher comments

X – improved the readability of his writing. Gaps between words and writing on the lines. He is now very keen to write independently almost to a point where he wants to write all the time rather than listen!

X – is much more willing to 'have a go' at sketching, colouring and presenting neatly. He is more confident in his own abilities e.g. he joined in with activities during camp which involved balance and tried to ride a bike. X now wants work to look good and when concentrating his presentation is much better.

X – is now doing joined-up writing and speed of copying has increased markedly. There was a big improvement in attitude and he wants to do well. X used to copy letter for letter and can now remember several letters in a row and therefore speed of writing is much faster. He is keen to present work neatly and insists on joined-up writing. I feel the benefits of the intervention programme will be even more evident when he applies his new skills to other curricular areas.

X – has a much more positive attitude overall and handwriting is more fluent and readable.

X – still holds his pen incorrectly (which may account for slow speed of work) but his presentation is excellent as is his attitude and handwriting.

X – has made a lot of progress in his curricular work. He is more co-ordinated and the presentation of his work has improved greatly. He can now space work out more easily and this helps with presentation.

X – work has improved a great deal in class. He is more capable now of completing some small tasks in an independent way.

X – I am pleased with the work that is now being produced in class. It is much neater and for the most part there is more motivation in terms of what can be produced.

X – obvious improvement in co-ordination, which is very noticeable during PE.

X – I noticed an immediate improvement in his posture. I had not seen him for several weeks and found it hard to believe the difference.

X – he has thoroughly enjoyed every minute of the programme and he has not missed a session. If I am running a little bit late he asks when it is going to be his turn.

The pupils at Elemore were committed to developing their skills and so proud of their achievements that they wanted their real names to be identified in this chapter. I take great delight at this stage acknowledging the efforts made by these individual pupils who are:

Tom, Danielle, Stephen G., Steven R., Leigh, Daniel, James, Jacqueline, Paul, Craig and Chris.

I thank them personally for their hard work, sustained effort and recommendations as to how the programme could be extended further.

Figures 9.2–9.5 are handwriting samples from two of the youngsters involved, showing differences before and after intervention. Unfortunately, it is not possible to include them all but they can be viewed if anyone has the opportunity to visit Elemore Hall. The project ran from October 1998 until July 1999 and during the final week as well as euphoria there were many tears. The majority of the youngsters had done so well that they were told that they did not need to attend the 'exercise groups' the following term. This in itself caused distress to a few. The pupils themselves then provided us with the solution for the future. They felt that their own competencies had developed to such an extent that they could offer support to younger pupils who would be admitted to the school in September 1999. From my previous studies working with secondary age pupils in a mainstream environment it was clear that the greatest benefit was the improvement in positive relationships between the youngsters themselves. At Elemore the pupils had discovered a means of helping each other: by becoming tutors themselves they would be able to develop still further their improving self-esteem while at the same time offering peer support to newly admitted youngsters who might be finding a new educational environment quite daunting.

During the last week of term the work of the staff and pupils was acknowledged formally and each child who had completed the two-term intervention was presented in front of the school, parents and guests, with a Certificate of Achievement. The programme is up and running this year (October 1999) and following the advice given by pupils, the successes will be as evident with the next pupils as they have been with those identified in this study.

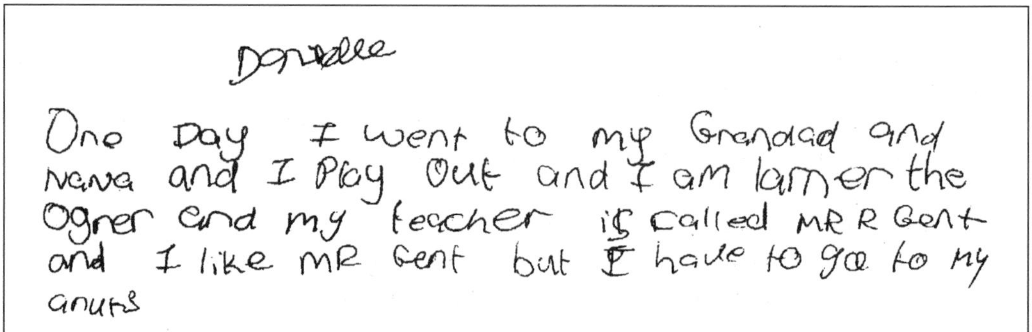
Danielle

One Day I went to my Grandad and
Nana and I Play Out and I am larner the
Ogrer and my teacher is called MR R Gent
and I like MR Gent but I have to goa to my
anuts

Figure 9.2 Handwriting sample Danielle, September 1998

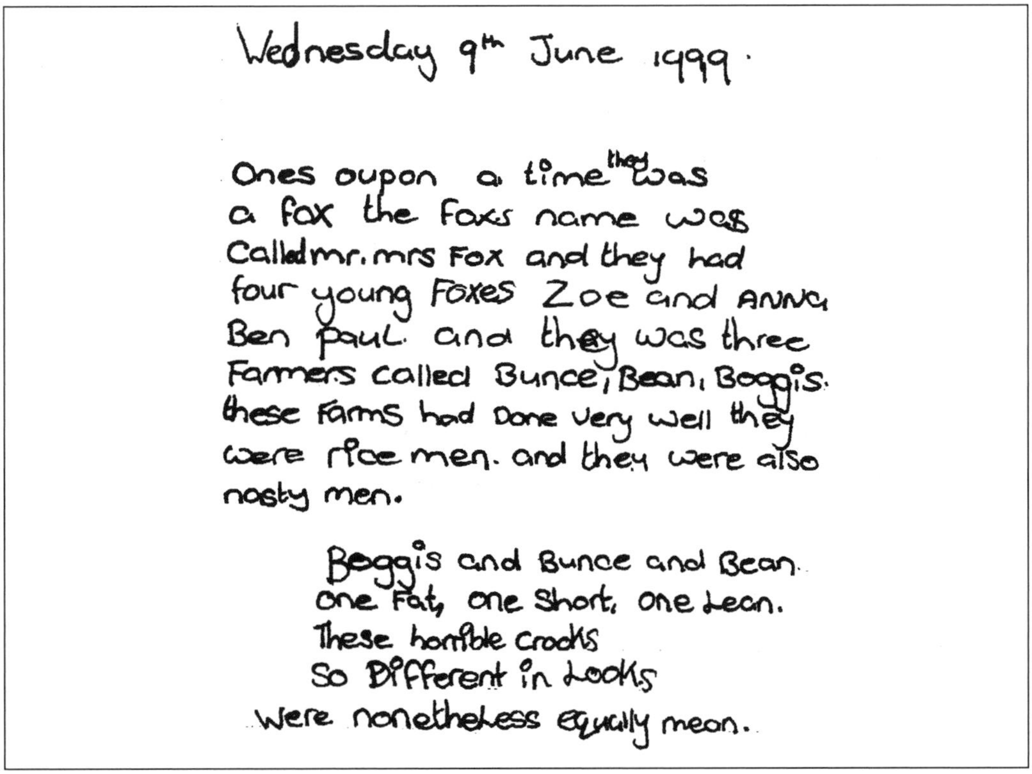

Wednesday 9th June 1999.

Ones oupon a time they was
a fox the foxs name was
Called mr. mrs Fox and they had
four young Foxes Zoe and Anna
Ben paul. and they was three
Farmers called Bunce, Bean, Boggis.
these farms had Done very well they
were rice men. and they were also
nasty men.

Boggis and Bunce and Bean.
one Fat, one Short, one Lean.
These horrible crooks
So Different in Looks
Were nonetheless equally mean.

Figure 9.3 Handwriting sample Danielle, June 1999

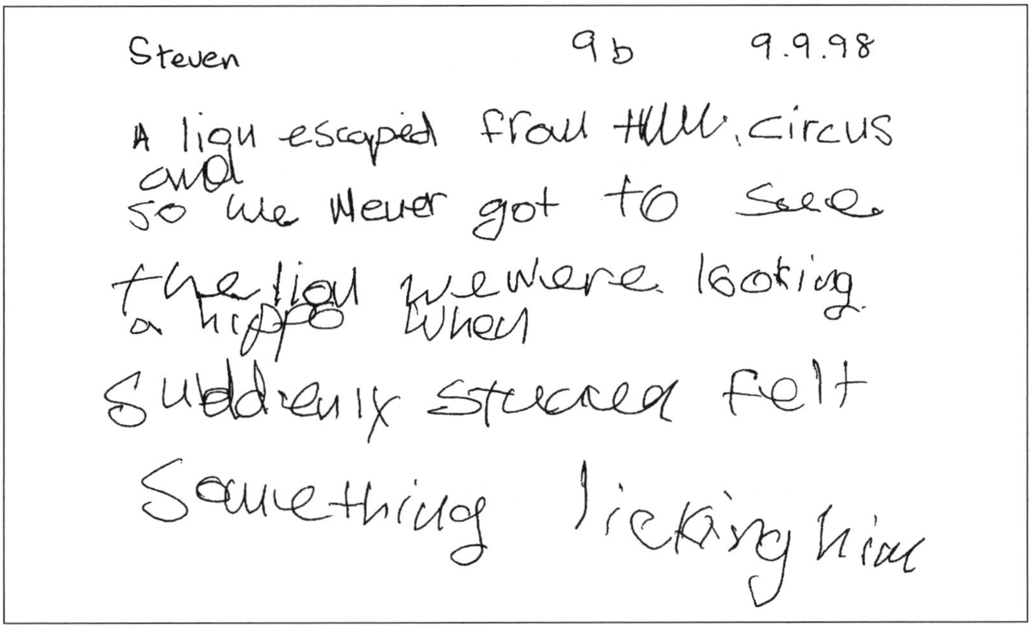

Steven   9 b   9.9.98

A lign escaped from the, circus
and
so we never got to see
the lign we were looking
a hippo when
suddenly steven felt
something licking him

Figure 9.4 Handwriting sample Steven, September 1998

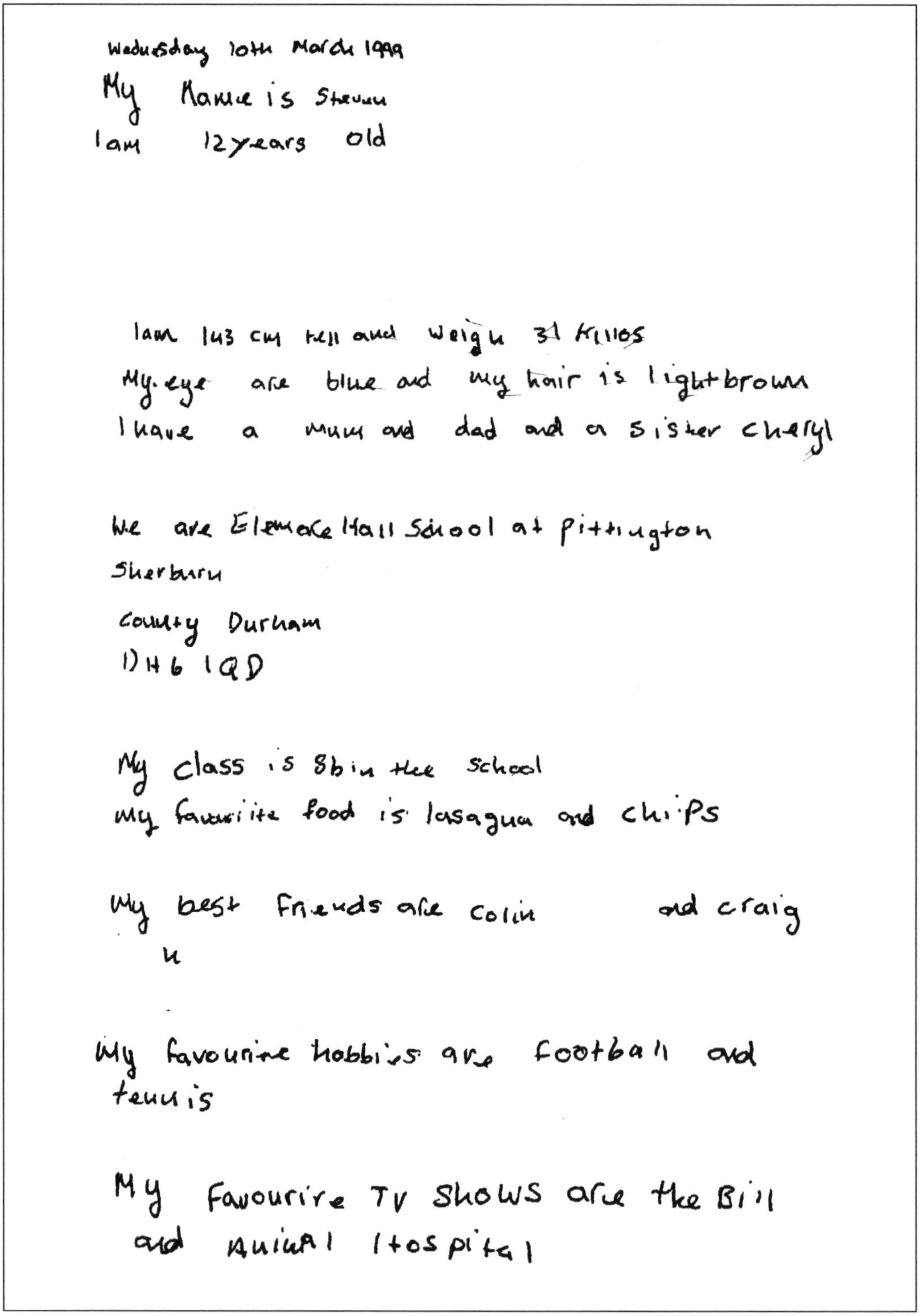

Wednesday 10th March 1999

My Name is Steven

I am 12 years old

I am 143 cm tell and weigh 31 Killos

My eye are blue and my hair is lightbrown

I have a mum and dad and a sister cheryl

We are Elemore Hall School at Pittiugton

Sherburn

County Durham

DH6 1QD

My class is 8b in the school

My favourite food is lasagua and chips

My best Friends are colin   and craig

        u

My favourite hobbies are football and

tennis

My Favourire Tv shows are the Bill

and Animal Hospital

Figure 9.5 Handwriting sample Steven, March 1999

I would like to conclude this chapter with the comment made by Barbara Barron when asked to give her impression of the intervention:

Any school which plans to undertake this work needs to be sure that the staff involved have sufficient time, on a daily basis, to do the exercises. In the early stages we were not aware of this commitment and it was difficult having to 'steal time' from our regular work. Additional time was then made available. For this we were very grateful.

The project has been very satisfying because we can see the positive results. How lovely to be able to intervene in a way so easy and enjoyable for both staff and pupils and get clear and effective results within two terms! Once the initial difficulty of finding time and space for the programme was solved, the day-to-day process of doing the exercises has been a real pleasure.

The pupils have all enjoyed the extra attention. Far from feeling stigmatised, the pupils in the project have felt part of an exclusive and enviable group. Going out to 'do exercises' is seen very positively. Pupils who are not involved in the project repeatedly asked to be allowed to come. We have given some small practical rewards and pupil commendation, but for the most part the exercise sessions have been sufficiently rewarding in themselves.

In such an educational environment where the youngsters have significant emotional and behavioural difficulties it is only realistic to recognise that some pupils will drop out of the project entirely for reasons beyond the school's control. Also some will lose many days because of ill health, poor behaviour or absconding. Even so, the experience at Elemore showed that two-thirds of those who started did complete the programme and the majority of those benefited enormously.

It could be hoped that those who were involved in absconding did so in a more co-ordinated manner!

The school welcomes enquiries from anyone seeking further information or hoping to set up a similar project. The contact address for Mike Davey, Head Teacher is: Elemore Hall School, Pittington, Sherburn, Co. Durham, DH6 1QD.

Chapter 10

The future

During the past ten years there have been great advances in the understanding of developmental dyspraxia. Those with symptoms of the condition were previously described as having 'Clumsy Child Syndrome' or 'Minimal Brain Dysfunction'. A 'diagnosis' can provide additional resources but more importantly, those working with the child will have a greater insight into the difficulties experienced. However, because dyspraxic children and adults don't look different from anyone else, those who are unaware of their difficulties do not make allowances. Wetton (1997) analysed videotapes of children in an early years setting. She observed that: 'Children who are ostensibly normal but are slightly "clumsy" or socially inept are not tolerated if they show any deviation from expected playing styles. Yet other children who have been statemented and have visible special needs are accepted.'

A child's feelings about himself reflect the opinions of his peers: criticism and rejection become the basis of the child's self-image. These negative experiences have a major influence on the child's emotional development and continue through to adulthood.

Children with dyspraxia find it difficult to make sense of what is going on around them. Learning new skills is so difficult and they don't know why. They frequently become the victims of bullying which creates further distress. Self-esteem and confidence are lowered still further and eventually the child finds he is totally incapable of meeting the demands of attending school.

This cycle of failure, which is seen in so many children, can be broken if parents and professionals are aware of the potential difficulties and provide positive experiences in an inclusive environment. This responsibility does not rest solely with educators: the child's relationships within the family must also be considered. The child may well be the focus of criticism from brothers and sisters: he may be the one perceived as demanding most attention from parents. 'Inclusion' should be practised in the home.

There is some debate among professionals as to the prevalence of developmental dyspraxia. When figures are quoted, e.g. 'As many as 10 per cent of the population may have dyslexia, 6 per cent dyspraxia, 5 per cent attention deficit and hyperactivity disorder' and so it goes on, it appears that more than 50 per cent of the population show evidence of some disorder! Obviously this is not the case because of the comorbidity of the conditions. Assessment may highlight the 'primary' disorder but appropriate support should be available to address all areas of concern. Where a child is identified with ADHD, medication (Ritalin – Methylphenidate) can have a dramatic effect on behaviour and concentration. This facilitates a more accurate assessment of the child's learning capabilities when 'specific' problems are then identified. Ongoing assessment and regular review is essential to provide the most appropriate learning environment.

One ten year old with whom I was recently involved was identified by school staff as having problems with co-ordination and additionally had struggled to acquire basic reading skills. He was given a structured motor skills programme and after six weeks his progress was reviewed. At the outset he had appeared to be equally unco-ordinated on both the left and right sides of the body. He could balance for only two seconds on either foot, was unable to hop and he could not direct a ball with either his left or right hand to within three metres of the target. When reassessed, William had developed much greater competence in his left side but there had been virtually no improvement in the right. Consequently, he was referred to the school medical officer and assessed by a consultant paediatrician. William was diagnosed with mild right-sided hemiplegia which was evident only because the staff in the school identified a motor difficulty, provided a structured PE programme and their experience from working with other children had shown them that William had not made the expected progress.

Figure 10.1 represents the systems which could be in place to identify and support children and adults with dyspraxia. To be effective, professionals must be aware of the presenting difficulties, and close liaison between Health, Education and other supporting agencies is essential.

Research

Comparisons are being made to consider whether the 'environment' affects the incidence of dyspraxia.

In Scandinavian countries, where great emphasis is placed on developing gross motor skills up to the age of seven, the incidence of dyspraxia is reported as only one to two per cent of the population. In Sweden, full-time state nursery education is available for children from 12 months of age. In recent years there has been a government initiative to take up sport. While incentives are offered to older pupils, encouragement is given to preschool provision where children have access to extensive outdoor play equipment.

Much research is focusing on the metabolic basis for learning difficulties as discussed in Chapter 2. Individual assessments of more than 400 children and young adults with dyspraxia suggests that as many as 18 per cent have a history of lactose intolerance, allergies to milk and wheat with eczema and asthma present before the age of 12 months. Parents have reported some success with exclusion diets and supplements such as cod liver and evening primrose oils. I am currently involved with the Highland Psychiatric Research Group which is analysing breath

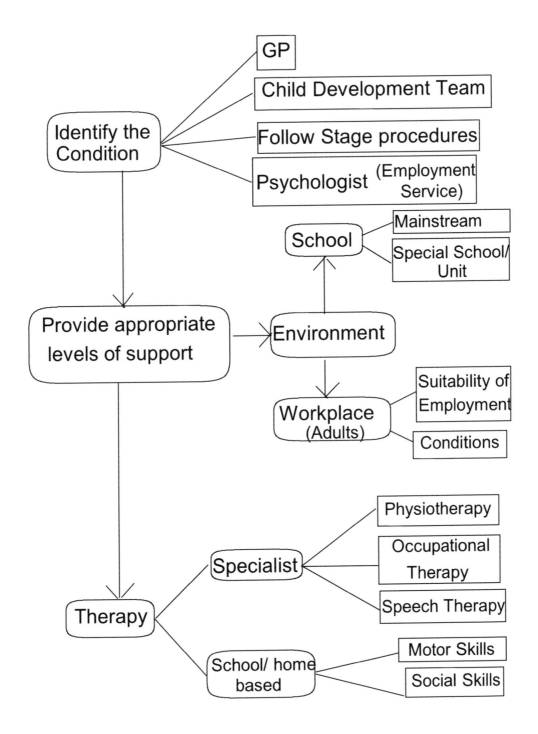

Figure 10.1 The network of support for children and adults diagnosed with dyspraxia

samples of youngsters where the underlying problem may be metabolic as opposed to neurological. When I ask parents and teachers if they notice anything specific about the child's breath it is surprising how many report a 'smell of sour milk'. It is still early days but perhaps in the not too distant future it will be possible to complete an even more comprehensive assessment which includes breath analysis.

Every day, as research evidence is published, more information becomes available about 'new' syndromes and disorders. While it is important to support children and adults with difficulties we must not seek to find a 'label' for everyone who may be slightly unco-ordinated, more outspoken or just a little different from the rest.

Appendix 1:
The Dyspraxia Foundation

The Dyspraxia Foundation is a national registered charity financed exclusively by voluntary contributions. It began in 1987 when Stella White and Marilyn Owen, two mothers of dyspraxic children, met at the 'Clumsy Group' clinic at the Great Ormond Street Hospital. They started a self-help group for families of youngsters with dyspraxia.

The demand for information from parents and professionals rapidly outstripped the abilities of such a group and the Dyspraxia Trust was founded. It was renamed the Dyspraxia Foundation in 1996 as the membership felt that this new title best described the structure and function of the organisation.

Appendix 2 includes fact sheets reproduced with permission from the Foundation which may be photocopied. Recommended reading and software materials appropriate for children and adults are available directly from the Foundation.

Dyspraxia Foundation,
8 West Alley,
Hitchin,
Herts SG5 1EG

Tel: 01462 454986 (Helpline)
Tel: 01462 455016 (Administration)
Fax: 01462 455052
Website: http://www.emmbrook.demon.co.uk/dysprax/homepage.htm

A comprehensive list of the Foundation's local co-ordinators is given as Appendix 3. A membership form for the Dyspraxia Foundation follows.

DYSPRAXIA FOUNDATION

'recognising developmental co-ordination disorders'

Membership of the Dyspraxia Foundation is open to anyone with an interest in dyspraxia. Each member receives 'Midline' (twice yearly), a copy of the Annual Review, interim newsletters, reduced rates for articles, books, conferences and events and the vital support of Adult and Local Groups.

The Dyspraxia Foundation also publishes 'Focus' a newsletter for and by adults with dyspraxia and DTN (Dyspraxia Teen News), a newsletter for and by affected teenagers.

MEMBERSHIP FORM
Please use BLOCK CAPITALS throughout

Title:...Initial:....................................

Surname:...

Road:...

Town: ....

County:..

Postcode: ....

Telephone No: (Daytime)..

              (Evening)..

Occupation: ....

I enclose my membership subscription of £20.00
I enclose my overseas membership subscription of £30.00 (Sterling)
I enclose an additional donation of
£30.00 £20.00 £10.00 Other
Cheques should be made payable to 'Dyspraxia Foundation'

Signed:...

For details of reduced membership fees, please contact our Hitchin office.

Subscriptions are renewable annually on 1st April.
Members joining after the 1st January will not be asked to pay a renewal subscription in the same calendar year.

We like to enable members to share their experiences. If you do not want your name and address passed to other members, please tick here ❑

Please return to: The Membership Secretary, Dyspraxia Foundation,
8 West Alley, Hitchin, Herts, SG5 1EG

Appendix 2: Dyspraxia Foundation publications

What is Developmental Dyspraxia?

Dyspraxia is an immaturity of the brain resulting in messages not being properly transmitted to the body. It affects at least 2 per cent of the population in varying degrees and 70 per cent of those affected are male. Dyspraxia is a disability but those affected do not look disabled. This is both an advantage and a disadvantage.

These are some of the problems caused by dyspraxia:

- Clumsiness
- Poor posture
- Walking awkwardly
- Confused about which hand to use
- Difficulties throwing or catching a ball
- Sensitivity to touch
- Find some clothes uncomfortable
- Poor short-term memory, they often forget tasks learned the previous day
- Poor body awareness
- Reading and writing difficulties
- Cannot hold a pen or pencil properly
- Poor sense of direction
- Cannot hop, skip or ride a bike
- Slow to learn to dress or feed themselves
- Cannot answer simple questions even though they know the answers
- Speech problems, slow to learn to speak or speech may be incoherent
- Phobias or obsessive behaviour
- Impatience
- Intolerance to having hair or teeth brushed, or nails and hair cut
- Plasters are uncomfortable to wear

Not all of these will apply to every dyspraxic individual, and many of these problems can be overcome in time, but also could be met by more problems.

Older children are usually verbally competent and converse well with adults. They may be ostracised by their own peer group because they do not fit in. They may cleverly avoid doing those tasks that are difficult or even impossible for them.

Dyspraxic people can be of average or above intelligence but are often behaviourally immature. They try hard to fit in to the socially acceptable norms when at school but often throw tantrums when at home. They may find it difficult to understand logic and reason.

Not all dyspraxic people have all of these problems, but all have a common link. Many parents will say that all of their children have some of these problems but if your child is dyspraxic, either diagnosed or not, you will know the difference between an ordinary child with any of these problems and a dyspraxic child.

There is no cure for dyspraxia but the earlier a child is treated then the greater the chance of improvement. Occupational therapists, physiotherapists and extra help at school can all help a dyspraxic child to cope or overcome many difficulties. Sadly, a lot of the skills that we take for granted will never become automatic to someone with dyspraxia and they will have to be taught these skills.

The Dyspraxia Foundation wishes to help all dyspraxic people and their families. We believe that promoting awareness will help people diagnosed as dyspraxic to be understood, which will in turn build up their self-esteem. We also know that there are a lot of dyspraxic children and adults who have gone unnoticed and we desperately want to let them know that there is a reason for their problems, and that they can get help or just meet and talk to other dyspraxic people.

Developmental Dyspraxia Explained

What is **Dyspraxia?** It is an impairment or immaturity of the organisations of movement: associated with this there may be problems of language, perception and thought.

Other Names. Clumsy Child Syndrome, Developmental Co-ordination Disorder (DCD), Perceptuo-motor Dysfunction, Minimal Brain Dysfunction, Motor Learning Difficulty.

Movement. Gross and fine motor skills are hard to learn, difficult to retain and generalise, and hesitant and awkward in performance.

Language. Articulation may be immature or even unintelligible in early years. Language may be impaired or late to develop.

Perception. There is a poor understanding of the messages that the senses convey and difficulty in relaying those messages to actions.

Thought. Dyspraxic children of average intelligence may have great difficulty in planning and organising thoughts. Those with moderate learning difficulties may have these problems to a greater extent.

Cause. For most children there is no known cause, although it is thought to be an immaturity of neurone development in the brain rather than brain damage. Dyspraxic children have no clinical neurological abnormality to explain their condition.

How would I recognise a dyspraxic child?

The preschool child

- History of lateness reaching milestones e.g. rolling over, sitting, walking and speaking.
- May not be able to run, hop or jump.
- Appears not to be able to learn anything instinctively but must be taught skills.
- Poor at dressing.
- Slow and hesitant in most actions.
- Poor pencil grip.
- Cannot do jigsaws or shape-sorting games.
- Art work is very immature.
- Has no understanding of in/on/behind/in front of etc.
- Unable to catch or kick a ball.
- Commonly anxious and distractible.
- Finds it difficult to keep friends or judge how to behave in company.

The school age child

- All the problems of the preschool child may still be present with little or no improvement.

- PE is avoided.
- The child does badly in class but significantly better on a one-to-one basis.
- Attention span is poor and the child reacts to all stimuli without discrimination.
- May have trouble with maths, reading and particularly spelling.
- Great difficulty may be experienced in copying from the blackboard.
- Writing is laborious and immature.
- Unable to remember and/or follow instructions.
- Generally poorly organised.

Where do I get help?

Preschool

Talk to your GP and Health Visitor. A referral should be made to a paediatrician or a child development centre. Assessment can then be made by a psychologist, physiotherapist, speech therapist and occupational therapist as is deemed appropriate.

School age children

Talk to your GP, School Nurse or School Doctor (appointments can be made through the school or local health centre), class teacher or the special needs co-ordinator as appropriate. For further information refer to the DfEE *Special Educational Needs: A Guide for Parents,* obtainable from the DfEE by telephoning 0171 925 5000. Hospital referral may be required for special tests or treatment.

What about the future?

Prognosis is usually hopeful in that, although dyspraxia is not curable, the child will improve in some areas with growing maturity. He/she can be helped to a large extent with the appropriate treatment and suitable leisure facilities to overcome the continuing problems that he/she will undoubtedly face.

Dyspraxia in Primary Schools

Dyspraxia is an impairment or immaturity of the organisation of movement. Associated with this there may be problems of language perception and thought. Dyspraxia is an immaturity in the way the brain processes information and this results in messages not being properly or fully transmitted. Estimates put the number of children experiencing the condition at between 2 and 10 per cent of the population. Boys are four times more likely to be affected than girls.

When youngsters enter the education system whether it is at the age of three in nursery class or at the age of four into reception class, parents may for the first time be able to discuss concerns about their child's development. The teacher or support assistant will be able to confirm that in relation to other youngsters of the same age, a particular child is finding certain tasks very difficult. Parents know their children better than any one else and will have seen evidence in the home environment of the problems the child is facing in school. If as a teacher, you are concerned about a child's development, speak to the parent as soon as possible and obtain relevant information about the child's achievement of early milestones.

The dyspraxic child may have displayed many of the symptoms listed below and some will have been evident before the age of three.

- Irritability at birth
- Poor feeding
- Poor sleeping
- Engages in high levels of motor activity, constantly waving arms and legs
- Slow to achieve milestones such as sitting (often after the age of eight months), crawling (some never crawl), walking, hopping, jumping, walking up and down stairs
- Constantly tripping and falling over
- Limited ability to concentrate on specific tasks and is easily distracted
- Unaware of external dangers e.g. jumping from a high wall or from the top of a climbing frame, walking towards a busy road
- Often frightened and will not climb on apparatus
- Delayed acquisition of language

A classroom observation will enable the teacher to determine whether there are certain activities which the child finds difficult or avoids. Areas which present particular difficulties to the child are:

- Development of perceptual skills (finds form boards, shape sorters and constructional toys difficult to assemble).
- Laterality is not yet established so the child will use the right hand to complete tasks on the right side of the body and the left hand to complete tasks on the left side.
- Games lessons/music and movement classes are often difficult. The child has difficulty with ball skills and other eye – hand and eye – foot co-ordination activities.

- Listening skills may be poor and the child may not respond to sequential commands.
- Immature social skills.

In addition to the above the following behaviours can be observed by the age of seven.

- Problems adapting to a structured school routine.
- Difficulties evident in PE: poor unco-ordinated movements.
- Slow at dressing (often look messy) – unable to tie shoe laces.
- Handwriting barely legible – immature drawings and poor copying skills.
- Literal use of language.
- Only able to remember two or three instructions either visually, verbally or both.
- Class work is completed slowly and is rarely finished.
- Continuing high levels of motor activity.
- Motor stereo types – hand flapping or clapping when excited.
- Easily distressed, very emotional.
- Messy eaters and have problems using a knife and fork.
- Often loners – have problems forming a relationship with other youngsters and appear isolated in the class group.
- The child may report physical symptoms – migraines, headaches, feeling sick.

If there is a child in your class who may be dyspraxic it is important that the social and educational environment is adapted to meet his/her needs

REMEMBER

- The child may need supervision and encouragement to stay on task.
- Seating should allow the child to rest both feet flat on the floor and the child should be encouraged to sit with upright posture.
- The desk should be at elbow height with a facility to use a sloping surface for reading and additional activities.
- The child should be placed so he/she is able to view the teacher directly without turning the body and be close enough to hear and see instructions. In addition, he/she should sit where there are minimal distractions e.g. away from windows or doors.
- Make prepared recording sheets available to reduce the quantity of handwriting required.
- Use lined paper with spaces sufficiently wide to accommodate the child's handwriting.
- Attach the paper to the desk to avoid the unnecessary distress of having to hold it in position with one hand while trying to draw or write with the other.
- Break down activities/tasks into small components.
- Reinforce verbal instructions by repeating several times and give no more than one or two instructions at one time.

- Assist with copying from the board by using different colour pens/chalks for every line or leave larger gaps after every three or four words.
- Allow extra time for completion of a task.
- Ensure that the child is given a great deal of encouragement and positive feedback.
- Be aware that during sudden growth spurts difficulties may become more apparent.
- Liaise with the relevant medical professionals for further advice in the classroom and PE setting.
- If the condition is identified early and provision made within the classroom then subsequent disaffection and reduction in self-esteem will be minimised.

Recommended reading

- *Praxis Makes Perfect II*
- *Developmental Dyspraxia: Identification and Intervention – A Manual for Parents and Professionals* by Madeleine Portwood
- *Dyspraxia – A Handbook for Therapists* by Michele Lee and Jenny French
  These publications are available from: Dyspraxia Foundation, 8 West Alley, Hitchin, Herts SG5 1EG.
  Tel: 01462 454986 (Helpline)
  Tel: 01462 455016 (Administration)
  Fax: 01462 455052
  Website: http://www.emmbrook.demon.co.uk/dysprax/homepage.htm

Dyspraxia in Secondary Schools

Dyspraxia is an impairment or immaturity of the organisation of movement. Associated with this there may be problems of language, perception and thought.

Dyspraxia is an immaturity in the way the brain processes information and this results in messages not being properly or fully transmitted. Estimates put the number of children experiencing the condition at between 2 and 10% of the population. Boys are four times more likely to be affected than girls.

In some cases dyspraxia is not identified until the child reaches secondary school. He/she may have managed to cope through their previous schools with only minor difficulties. However the structure of secondary schools may prove to be too difficult for the child. It is at this point that problems manifest themselves especially in view of the organisational skills that are required in secondary education. If dyspraxia is not identified and the child enters secondary education there can be such a high incidence of low self-esteem and disaffection that behavioural difficulties are evident.

What to look for:

- Difficulties with physical activities such as in PE with the child having difficulty with eye – hand and eye – foot co-ordination (e.g. ball skills), running or using equipment easily.
- Poor posture, body awareness and awkward movements.
- Confusion over laterality with the pupil interchanging between left and right hand for different tasks.
- Poor short-term visual and verbal memory – copying from the board, dictation, following instructions.
- Writing difficulties both with style and speed – frequently children have an awkward pen grip.
- Poorly developed organisational skills and difficulty with planning essays.
- Activities which involve well developed sequencing abilities are difficult.
- Problems with awareness of time, pupils need constant reminders.
- Often have poor exercise tolerance, tire easily and may require longer periods of rest and sleep.
- Some children nay have phobias, obsessive or immature behaviour.
- Sensitive to external stimulation e.g. different levels of light, sound or heat intensity. Extremes of emotions: highly excitable at times and evidence of significant mood swings.
- Lack of awareness of potential danger, particularly relevant to practical and science subjects.
- Often loners and have limited development of social skills.

Is there a dyspraxic child in your class?

Remember:

- Give the child as much encouragement as possible and make sure they are not made to feel a failure.

- Be aware of their difficulties and give strategies to reduce the frustration they experience, particularly when required to complete written work.
- Break down activities and tasks into smaller components.
- Teach the child strategies in order to help them remember and organise themselves (e.g. use of diaries and lists).
- Assist with short-term verbal memory tasks by not giving too many words in dictation and asking the child to repeat instructions to you.
- Help with short-term visual memory tasks by not expecting the child to be able to copy large blocks of text. Use strategies to help with copying from the board by using different colours per line or giving a ruler to copy text for each line. If demonstrating activities, break down the tasks into stages and give a few at a time.
- Allow the child to finish a task before moving on: they will feel a failure when work is continually left incomplete.
- In PE/games gain advice from the medical professionals and ensure that if the child is unable to join in a team game he/she is given activities that will build up their particular abilities. Where possible allow the child alternatives from taking part in team games where the child will be identified as letting his/her side down.
- Ensure that, where required, assistance is given to the pupil to find his/her way around: they may forget where they are supposed to be.
- Allow access to word processor/lap-tops/palm tops if they are available – a voice processor with at least 80% accuracy can be invaluable.
- It is important to work with parents as they know their child better than anyone else.
- Ensure that there is good liaison with medical professionals.
- Be aware that during sudden growth spurts difficulties may manifest themselves to a greater extent.
- Encourage a close relationship with another child who can act as a guide/helper especially for the first few months following transfer to secondary school.
- Ensure that all instructions are always clear and precise. Make sure you explain yourself fully even if this means stating the obvious as they may not understand sarcasm or irony.

With the right support, encouragement and help dyspraxic children do well at school.

Further reading

Praxis Makes Perfect II

Developmental Dyspraxia: Identification and Intervention – A Manual for Parents and Professionals by Madeleine Portwood

Dyspraxia – A Handbook for Therapists by Michelle Lee and Jenny French

These publications are available from:

Dyspraxia Foundation: 8 West Alley, Hitchin, Herts SG5 1EG

Tel: 01462 454986 (Help-line)   Tel: 01462 455016 (Administration)

Fax: 01462 455052

Web-site: http://www.emmbrook.demon.co.uk/dysprax/homepage.htm

Dyspraxia – A Guide for Students in Further and Higher Education

In many ways the conditions of dyspraxia and dyslexia coexist and often coexist in the same person. Dyspraxia is an impairment of the organisation of movement that is often accompanied by problems with language, perception and thought. Dyslexia is primarily a difficulty with learning to read, write and spell and is also generally accompanied by other problems such as poor organisational abilities. The pattern of difficulties in dyspraxia (or Developmental Co-ordination Disorder) may vary widely from person to person as with dyslexia.

A dyspraxic student may have difficulties with:

Planning their movements and being aware of the space around them: They frequently bump into and trip over things. They may have a clumsy posture and poor muscle tone.

Perception: They find it difficult to judge heights and distances: This can make them appear clumsy.

Co-ordinating different parts of the body: They may find it hard to catch, throw, and balance as well as moving the different parts of their body without looking. Sport and dancing can cause acute problems.

Laterality: It may be difficult to work out right from left without a reminder.

Manual and practical work: They may find it difficult to handle safely and easily keyboards, tools, cars, bandages, laboratory and cooking equipment, etc. They tend to knock over and spill things.

Handwriting: They tend to write laboriously slowly and/or untidily and illegibly. Accurate copying may be difficult.

Language: They may find it difficult to pronounce some words and may stutter.

Concentration: They may take a long time to complete a task and find it difficult to do more than one thing at a time.

Short-term memory and sequencing tasks: They may find it hard to make sense of information when listening to or reading instructions, taking notes from books and lecturers, and dealing with maps and charts. They may keep forgetting and losing things as well as finding it difficult to spell.

Organisation and thought: They may operate in a muddled way, having little sense of direction, time or space. They may constantly miss appointments and hand assignments in late because they find it difficult to organise themselves and their work. They may find it difficult to express themselves easily.

Response to external stimulation: They may be over or under sensitive to noise, touch, light and taste.

All the above can lead to **Emotional Problems,** making them easily depressed, angry, frustrated and anxious. Many have low self-esteem. This is particularly true if they have not received an early diagnosis and/or support. They can find it difficult to relate to others especially in groups and to read social cues correctly. These difficulties will become more apparent in times of stress for example during and before embarking on a new project. They also tend to be inconsistent and have 'good and bad days'.

Strategies that can be adopted by the College

1. Some students will have recently undergone cognitive assessments by educational and clinical psychologists. Those that have not should be encouraged to do so. This will make it easier to decide what additional resources a student will require, e.g. assistance with note-taking and being given extra time.

2. Most students will need counselling to determine their ability to successfully complete a course of study and advice regarding the suitability of a course for their vocational goals.

3. Tutors will need to give guidance in the planning and organisation of academic and practical work. The student will benefit from seeing examples of essays, reports and projects. Learning processes should be broken down into steps to allow opportunities for checking the student's understanding.

4. Strategies to compensate for poor memory and organisational skills should be available, e.g. the use of mnemonics, work timetables, flow charts and mind maps, handouts and word processors.

5. Training in relaxation techniques, assertiveness and confidence building would be beneficial in many cases.

6. If the course is of a practical nature, strategies should be in place to see that students can handle equipment such as cooking and laboratory equipment safely. Items that can be secured should be in order to stop spillage and breakage.

They should ideally be allowed extra time for their course work and be entitled to it for exams. They should have access to either a word processor or somebody to take their notes and write for them if necessary as well as general tuition support.

Students with dyspraxia or DCD in full time education can also claim Disabled Students Allowance – a lump sum with which the student can pay for equipment or services, e.g. to buy a tape recorder and/or for photocopying and specialist tuition. They should also be able to apply to the College's access fund for further funding.

Further reading

Perceptuo-motor Difficulties – Theory and Strategies to Help Children, Adolescents and Adults by Dorothy Penso. Published by Chapman and Hall, 1993.

Further information available from:

Mary Colley (Adult Co-ordinator), 7 Sumatra Road, London NW6 1PS Tel 020 7435 5443

Denise Jones (Adult Newsletter Editor) Tel 01203 743991

Skill (National Bureau for Students with Disabilities), 3rd Floor, Chapter House, 18 – 20 Crucifix Lane, London SEI 3JW Tel 0800 3285050

Adults with Dyspraxia

Getting a diagnosis

If you want a valid diagnosis, you should see a neurologist and/or an educational or clinical psychologist who specialises in specific learning difficulties. These can be seen privately or through your GP on the NHS. If you are applying for disability benefits, it is necessary to obtain a diagnosis from a chartered medical professional.

How can I find someone in my area who can diagnose me?

1.   Contact the Dyspraxia Foundation help line. Mary Colley, the Adult Co-ordinator, will do her best to help you.
2.   Contact your local Community Health Council. You can get the number in your phone directory.
3.   Ring round your local hospitals asking for the appropriate department.
4.   Contact your local Dyspraxia Foundation group or the Dyspraxia Foundation office in Hitchin.

How can I get a diagnosis from the NHS?

This can be difficult because the problems for adults who have dyspraxia are only starting to be recognised. To get a referral you should see your GP, who may be reluctant to take your concerns seriously. Before going, it is advisable to arm yourself with some of the names of appropriate specialists either from the adult help line or your Community Health Council. Your GP may not have this information or have the time to do the appropriate research. Go to your GP with a list of difficulties and make him/her understand how important a diagnosis is to you. You could take a friend or relative with you. If there are no specialists in your area, you have the right to be referred to another part of the country.

   If your GP has a fund holding practice, he/she might be willing to refer you to a private specialist and pay the fee for you. If the GP is not a fund holder, he can refer you to an NHS specialist or a private one where you will have to pay the fee.

Will I need further assessment and treatment?

An assessment by a chartered physiotherapist or occupational therapist will tell you exactly what your difficulties are and may suggest the most appropriate treatment. This could be a series of exercises and strategies for coping in your particular case. As with diagnosis, assessment is not easy to get from the NHS. The adult help line has a list of occupational therapists (mainly private) or you could approach your local Community Health Council or hospital. It is probably never too late for occupational therapy, though treatment might take longer if you are older.

Madeleine Portwood, a Senior Specialist Educational Psychologist, is at present working on an exercise programme for adults that is achieving positive results. (See the book list.)

Apart from physical treatments, counselling and psychological treatment can be of great help especially in combating the lack of self-esteem caused in many cases by not being able to do the simplest tasks. Drugs such as antidepressants can also be of help as well as complementary therapies, e.g. aromatherapy.

How would I know if I might be dyspraxic?

Below are the main indications of adult dyspraxia. This is not in any way meant to replace diagnosis by a doctor or other professional. Nobody, of course, will have all the characteristics. Core problems from a diagnostic point of view must lie in the areas of planning movement (gross motor skills and hand – eye co-ordination) though difficulties may occur in other areas too. Adults with dyspraxia may have some very positive characteristics. These may include strong intelligence, resilience and determination that has helped them overcome their difficulties.

Difficulties

Planning and movement (Gross motor skills)

- **Clumsy gait** and movement, difficulty changing direction, stopping and starting. Poor quality and control of movement.
- Poor posture, **poor muscle tone and strength** (especially pelvis and shoulders – generally floppy) reduced stamina.
- **Overflow and exaggerated accessory movements**.
- **Lack of awareness of body positioning in space**.
- Late at reaching milestones e.g. sitting, crawling, standing and walking (might not have crawled at all).
- **Tendency to fall, trip over and bump into things**.
- **Poor co-ordination**, difficulty riding a bike and driving a car.
- **Poor balance** and body control, difficulty holding a position.
- **Difficulty with sport, especially bat and ball games, working in teams**.
- **Lack of rhythm** e.g. with dancing, aerobics and playing musical instruments.
- Difficulties walking up and down hills.

Hand – eye co-ordination (Fine motor skills)

- **Lack of manual dexterity** e.g. unscrewing things, sewing, locks and keys, art and craft work, keyboard work, mechanical things, domestic chores (untidy) and DIY.
- **Handwriting** (poor pen grip, may not finish off words, keep on the line and/or may press too hard).

- Poor personal appearance, difficulties with make-up and doing hair, shabby clothes, tendency to look messy.
- Co-ordination problems with eating and drinking.

Perception

- Poor perception of messages and difficulty in relating these messages into actions.
- **Difficulty following instructions**. NOT instinctive: has to be taught everything step by step.
- **Little sense of time, direction, speed or weight**, poor map reading.
- Poor laterality and crossing the mid-line – discriminating right from left.
- Overly or unduly sensitive to noise, touch, taste, temperature or light.
- Tracking problems – lose place easily when reading.

Language

- Late learning to talk, continuous talking, repetition, clumsy immature speech, uncontrolled pitch and volume.

Thought and memory

- People with dyspraxia may have difficulty **planning** and **organising** their **thoughts**. They might find it hard to discriminate. They can be messy and cluttered, **unfocused** and erratic.
- They can have **accuracy problems** and find it hard to copy and proof-read. They often have **poor memory** (especially **short-term**) and may keep **forgetting and losing things**.
- They may find it **hard to concentrate**, only being able to do one thing at a time. **Slow to finish a task** if they do at all.
- Dyspraxia has links with **ADD** (Attention Deficit Disorder) and hyperactivity. Dyspraxic people may daydream and wander about aimlessly.
- Many will have dyslexia as well and have **problems** with reading, spelling, note taking, essay writing, and doing **maths** and **sequencing**.

Social and emotional problems

- Tendency to be easily frustrated, have emotional outbursts and to be **impulsive. Difficulties with listening**, especially in a large group. May find it difficult to pick up non-verbal signals and judge the tone or pitch of voice in themselves and others. Can take things too literally, be tactless, and interrupt, wanting immediate satisfaction. Can play the clown. Can be slow to adapt to new situations and to learn new skills.

- Can have problems with team work and have a tendency to take evasive action when they face a difficult situation.
- May be insomniac, stressed, depressed, anxious and indecisive. May have phobias, fears and obsessions.
- This may lead to a **lack of self-esteem** and difficulties being assertive. Can also be **individualistic** and **original**.

So am I dyspraxic?

You might be saying now 'doesn't everybody have many of the characteristics mentioned here', but with dyspraxia, it is the rule rather than the exception and some of these difficulties may be more severe than expected.

In order to make our voices heard and to offer support and help where it is needed, it is vital that you join our group and challenge the status quo.

Contact Mary Colley 7 Sumatra Road, London NW6 1PS Tel 020 7435 5443.

or

Dyspraxia Foundation 8 West Alley, Hitchin, Herts SG5 1EG.

Tel: 01462 454986

Fax: 01462 455052

Support agencies

CITIZEN'S ADVICE BUREAU. See telephone directory for your local office. (Provides an advocacy service for the disabled and disadvantaged. Can also advise on employment and rights for the disabled.)

THE DISABILITY LAW SERVICE Room 241 2nd Floor Bedford Row, London WCIR 4LR Tel. 020 7831 8031 (Advises on education, benefits, employment and community care.)

BENEFIT ENQUIRY LINE: Freephone 0800 882200. (For advice about benefits).

CITIZEN'S ADVOCACY INFORMATION AND TRAINING Unit 2k, Leroy House, Essex Rd, London N1 (Provides list of citizen's advocates and related schemes all over the country. These advocates are volunteers who help and stand up for the disabled and disadvantaged people in all areas of life.)

PACT (Placement Assessment and Counselling Team) – information available from your local employment office. They will investigate and note any problems you might have in work or when seeking work.

SKILL (National Bureau for students with disabilities) 336 Brixton Road, London 5W9 7AA Tel. 0800 3285050. (Advice about all aspects of post-16 education, training and employment for students with disabilities.)

BASIC SKILLS AGENCY (Head Office) Commonwealth House 1–19 Oxford St., London WC1A 1NU Tel. 020 7405 4017 and Free phone 0800 700987 (National Telephone Referral Service). (Basic skills are defined as the ability to read, write and speak in English and use mathematics at a level necessary to function and progress at work and in society in general. It runs regional campaigns to encourage adults to join basic skills programmes as well as helping children in conjunction with other agencies.)

DYSLEXIA INSTITUTE (Head Office) 153 Gresham Road, Staines, Middx. Tel. 01784 463851 (Will give you the name or your nearest institute where you can be assessed for both dyslexia and dyspraxia.)

AFASIC 347 Central Markets, Smithfield, London ECIA Tel. 020 7236 3832. (A group set up to help people under 25 with speech and language impairment.)

RADAR 12 City Forum, 250 City Road, London EC1V 8AF Tel. 020 7250 3222. (They publish information on services for disabled people including education and employment.)

MENCAP (Head Office) 123 Golden Lane, EC1 Tel. 020 7454 0454 or see the telephone book for your local office. (Mencap supports people with learning difficulties and in some area runs Pathways Employment Services, a job-finding agency for the disabled.)

UK ADVOCACY NETWORK (UKAN) Tel. Sheffield (0114) 2728171. (They should be able to put you in touch with your local advocacy service in your area if there is one.)

MIND (Info line) 0181 522 1728. (They will put you in touch with your local office that runs services to support people with mental difficulties.)

Recommended reading

Perceptuo–motor Difficulties and Strategies to Help Children, Adolescents and Adults by Dorothy Penso, Chapman and Hall (1993) £18.99. Concentrates mainly on adolescents and adults – a practical guide to everyday living.

Developmental Dyspraxia: Identification and Intervention – A Manual for Parents and Professionals by Madeleine Portwood. (Available from the Dyspraxia Foundation), price £15.50. This book provides a series of assessments and exercises for dyspraxia that can be carried out by non-professionals and which can be helpful for adults as well as children.

Handwriting Help-line – A guide for parents, teachers, adults and children with handwriting difficulties by Jean Alston and Jane Taylor £4.95. (Available from the Dyspraxia Foundation.)

ADD in Adults by Dr Gordon Serfontein, Simon and Schuster (Australia 1994). Strategies for coping with concentration and organisational problems which many adults with dyspraxia have.

Appendix 3: List of local Dyspraxia Foundation co-ordinators

Area	Contact	Telephone
ADULT CO-ORDINATOR	Mary Colley Mary will put people in touch with local adult co-ordinators	020 7435 5443
BERKSHIRE	Shirley McCaig	0118 941 8561
and/or	Barbara Royall	0118 941 1183
BRISTOL & BATH	Jill Tyler	0117 939 1740
CHESHIRE	Wendy Green	01606 784628
CLEVELAND	Debbie McGloin	01642 476726
COUNTY DURHAM	Tina Wilson	0191 384 8283
DERBYSHIRE	Kim Bannon	01246 557492
DEVON & CORNWALL	Linda Boardman	01803 867683
DORSET	Pauline Yates	01202 731242
GLOUCESTER	Linda Little	01242 672475
HERTFORDSHIRE	Janette Downey	01279 834040
HULL	Jacqui Ryan	01482 806422
KENT	Paul Bennington	01634 723728
LANCASHIRE	Ken Hummer	01253 738679
LEICESTERSHIRE	Julie & Derek Jearurn	0116 291 5669
LONDON (North)	June Gray	020 8527 6456
LONDON (South)	Liam Dillon	020 8674 9832
MANCHESTER (inc. Stockport)	Frances Shawcross	0161 485 4806

Area	Contact	Telephone
MILTON KEYNES	Isobelle Madden	01908 675290
NORTHERN IRELAND	Lorna Blackburn	01232 283098
NOTTINGHAMSHIRE	Anne Taylor (office)	01623 758459 0115 963 2220
OXFORDSHIRE	Marianne Moxon	01865 515344
SHROPSHIRE	Margaret Jolly	01743 873925
SOMERSET	Kim Ball	01373 451348
and/or	Helen Reynolds	01373 451104
SUSSEX	Kim Hobson	01273 707734 Fax: 01273 707735
TYNE AND WEAR	Office	0191 200 5100
WALES (Gwent)	Joan Shepperd	01633 856180
WALES (Cardiff)	Bernadette Guy	01222 615464
WEST MIDLANDS	Helen Stone	0121 422 6089 6.00–8.00pm weekdays
YORKSHIRE (West)	Caroline Lumley	01422 823327
YORKSHIRE (York)	Sue Large	01904 765357
SCOTLAND (regional)	Graham Robertson	01383 736814
EAST LOTHIAN	Audrey Berg	01875 812539
GLASGOW AND LANARKSHIRE	June Hamilton	01698 854382

Appendix 4: Useful names and addresses

Contacts

Speech Therapy Department
Nuffield Centre
Royal National Throat Nose & Ear
Hospital
Grays Inn Road
London WC1X 8EE, U.K.
Tel: 020 7915 1300

Youth Sport Trust
Loughborough University,
Loughborough,
Leicestershire,
LE11 3TU, U.K.
Tel: 01509 263171

Davies The Sports People,
Novara House,
Ashby Park,
Ashby de la Zouch,
Leicestershire, LE65 1NG, U.K.
Tel 0115 945 2203

Support Organisations

Dyspraxia Association of Ireland
Capri
5 Blackglen Court
Sandyford
Dublin 18
Ireland, U.K.
http://indigo.ie./~dyspraxi/

British Dyslexia Association
The National Organisation for Specific
Learning Difficulties,
98 London Road,
READING,
RG1 5AU, U.K.
voice: (0118) 966 2677
fax: (0118) 935 1927
http://www.bda-dyslexia.org.uk/

British Dyslexia Institute
133 Gresham rd.
Staines
Middlesex
TW18 2AJ, U.K.
Tel: 01784 463851
Fax: 01784 460747
http://www.dyslexia-inst.org.uk/

British Dyslexics
Tel: 01244 815552 – Information Pack
Tel: 01244 822884 – Help/Advice
Tel: 01244 816683 – General
Information
http://www.dyslexia.uk.com

Dyslexia 2000 Network
Adult Dyslexia Organisation,
336 Brixton Road,
London,
SW9 7AA,
U.K.
voice: 020 7924 9559
fax: 020 7274 7840
email: dyslexia.hq@dial.pipex.com
web: DYSLEXIA 2000 NETWORK

**British Institute for Learning
Disabilities**
Wolverhampton Road
Kidderminster
Worcs
DY10 3PP, U.K.
Tel: 01562 850251
Fax: 01562 851970
http://www.bild.org.uk/

ADDNet UK - ADHD
Tel: 020 8269 1400 or
Tel: 020 8516 1413 for local support
group
http://www.web-tv.co.uk/addnet.html

National Autistic Society
393 City Road,
London,
EC1V 1NG, U.K.
Tel: 020 7833 2299
Fax: 020 7833 9666
Email: nas@nas.org.uk

**The Centre for Social and
Communication Disorders,**
Elliot House,
113 Masons Hill,
Bromley,
Kent
BR2 9HT, U.K.
Tel. 020 8466 0098

Autism Research Unit
School of Health Sciences
University of Sunderland
Sunderland, SR2 7EE, U.K.
Tel: 0191 510 8922
Fax: 0191 510 8922
http://osiris.sunderland.ac.uk/aut-
cgi/homepage.htm

Apraxia - Kids
A parent support grouop for parents
of children with apraxia of speech
and or developmental verbal
dyspraxia.
http://www.jump.net/~gmikel/apraxia/

**National Center for Learning
Disabilities**
381 Park Avenue S,
Suite 1420,
New York,
New York 10016, U.S.
voice: (212) 545-7510
fax: (212) 545-9665

**Learning Disabilities Association
of America**
4156 Library Road
Pittsburgh,
Pennsylvania 15234, U.S.
voice: (412) 341-1515
fax: (412) 344-0224
email: idanatl@usaor.net
web: LDA Web Site

Orton Dyslexia Society
International Office
8600 La Salle Road
Chester Building,
Suite 382
8600 La Salle Road,
Baltimore,
Maryland 21286-2044, U.S.
messages: (800) ABCD123
voice: (800) 222-3123
voice: (410) 296-0232
fax: (410) 321-5069
email: ODS@pie.org
web: Orton Dyslexia Society Web Site

Dyslexia Research Center
4745 Centerville Road
Tallahassee,
Florida 32308, U.S.
voice: (904) 893-2216
fax: (904) 893-2440

**TALK: Taking Action Against
Language Disorders for Kids**
22980 Donna Lane,
Bend,
Oregon 97701
(503) 389-0004, U.S.

**Recording for the Blind and
Dyslexic**
20 Roszel Road,
Princetown,
New Jersey 08540, U.S.
voice: (609) 452-0606
fax: (609) 520-7990
email: webmaster@rfbd.org
web: Recording for the Blind and
Dyslexic

References

Allen, D.A. (1989) 'Developmental language disorders in preschool children: Clinical subtypes and syndromes', *School Psychology Review* **18**, 442–451.

Allen, M.H., Lincoln, A.J. and Kaufman, A.S. (1991) 'Sequential and simultaneous processing abilities of high-functioning autistic and language-impaired children', *Journal of Autism and Developmental Disorders* **21**, 483–502.

American Psychiatric Association (1994) *Diagnostic and Statistical Manual of Mental Disorders* (4th edn). Washington, DC: A.P.A.

Anastopoulos, A.D., Spisto, M.A. & Maher, M.C. (1994) 'The WISC-III freedom from distractibility factor: Its utility in identifying children with attention deficit hyperactivity disorder', *Psychological Assessment* **6**, 368–371.

Anderson, P. and Rourke, B.P. (1995) 'Williams syndrome', in Rourke, B.P. (ed.) *Syndrome of Non-verbal Learning Disabilities: Neurodevelopmental Manifestations* (pp. 138–170). New York: Guilford Press.

Aram, D.M. and Eisele, J.A. (1994) 'Limits of a left hemisphere explanation for specific language impairment', *Journal of Speech and Hearing Research* **37**, 824–830.

Aram, D.M., Ekelman, B.L. and Nation, J.E. (1984) 'Preschoolers with language disorders: 10 years later', *Journal of Speech and Hearing Research* **27**, 232–244.

Ayres, A.J. (1972) *Sensory Integration and Learning Disorders.* Los Angeles, California: Western Psychological Services.

Barber, M.A., Milich, R., Welsh, R. (1996) 'Effects of reinforcement schedule and task difficulty on the performance of attention deficit hyperactivity disordered boys and a control group', *Journal of Clinical Child Psychology* **25**, 66–76.

Barkley, R.A. (1990) *Attention Deficit Hyperactivity Disorder: A Handbook for Diagnosis and Treatment.* New York: Guilford Press.

Barkley, R.A. (1997) 'Behavioural inhibition, sustained attention, and executive functions: Constructing a unifying theory of ADHD', *Psychological Bulletin* **121**(01), 65–94.

Barkley, R.A., DuPaul, G.J. and McMurray, M.B. (1991) 'Attention deficit disorder with and without hyperactivity: Clinical response to three dose levels of methylphenidate', *Paediatrics* **87**, 519–531.

Barkley, R.A., Murphy, K.R., Kwasnik, D. (1996) 'Psychological adjustment and adaptive impairments in young adults with ADHD', *Journal of Attention Disorders* **1**, 41–54.

Benton, D. *et al.* (1995) 'The impact of long-term vitamin supplementation on cognitive function', *Psychopharmacology* **117**, 298–305.

Benton, D. *et al.* (1997) 'Thiamine supplementation for mood and cognitive functioning', *Psychopharmacology* **129**, 66–71.

Biederman, J., Newcorn, J. and Sprich, S.E. (1991) 'Comorbidity of attention deficit hyperactivity disorder with conduct, depressive, anxiety, and other disorders', *American Journal of Psychiatry* **148**, 564–577.

Bishop, D.V.M. (1992) 'The underlying nature of specific language impairment', *Journal of Child Psychology, Psychiatry, and Allied Disciplines* **33**, 3–66.

Bishop, D.V.M., North T. and Donlan, C. (1995) 'Genetic basis of specific language impairment: Evidence from a twin study', *Development Medicine and Child Neurology* **37**, 56–71.

Buzan, T. (1977) *Use Both Sides of Your Brain.* New York: Dutton.

Carramazza, A. *et al.* (1976) 'Right-hemisphere damage and verbal problem solving behaviour', *Brain and Language* **3**, 41–6.

Code, C. (1987) *Language, Aphasia and the Right Hemisphere.* Chichester: John Wiley.

Cohen, M.J., Krawiecki, N. and DuRant, R.H. (1987) 'The neuropsychological approach to the remediation of dyslexia', *Archives of Clinical Neuropsychology* **2**, 163–173.

Coltheart, M. (1983) 'The right hemisphere and disorders of reading', in Young, A.W. (ed.) *Functions of the Right Cerebral Hemisphere.* London: Academic Press.

Connors, C.K. and Wells, K.C. (1986) *Hyperactive Children: A Neuropsychosocial Approach.* Beverley Hills, CA: Sage.

Courchesne, E. (1991) 'Neuroanatomic Imaging in Autism', *Paediatrics 87:* 781–790.

Cratty, B.J. (1994) *Clumsy Child Syndromes: Descriptions, Evaluations and Remediation.* Langhorn, PA: Harwood Academic Publishers.

Crawford, M. (1996) 'The role of essential fatty acids in neural development: Implications for perinatal nutrition', *American Journal Clinical Nutrition* **57**, 703S–710S.

Department for Education and Employment (1997) *Excellence for All Children.* London: The Stationery Office.

Dewey, D. and Kaplan, B.J. (1992) 'Analysis of praxis task demands in the assessment of children with developmental motor deficits', *Developmental Neuropsychology* **8**, 367–379.

Durham LEA (1998) *Special Educational Needs: Assessment and Provision. A Guide for Professionals.* Durham County Council.

Edelman, G.M. (1989) *Neural Darwinism. The Theory of Neuronal Group Selection.* Oxford: Oxford University Press.

Edelman, G.M. (1992) *Bright Air, Brilliant Fire on the Matter of Mind.* London: A. Lane Publishers.

Eisele, J.A. and Aram, D.M. (1993) 'Differential effects of early hemisphere damage on lexical comprehension and production', *Aphasiology* **5**, 513–523.

Ellis, A.W. (1982) 'Spelling and writing (and reading and speaking)', in Ellis, A.W. (ed.) *Normality and Pathology in Cognitive Functions.* London: Academic Press.

Ellis, A. and Young, A. (1988) *Human Cognitive Neuropsychology.* Hillsdale, NJ: Lawrence Erlbaum Associates.

Farquharson, J., Cherry, E.C., Abbasi, K.A., Patrick, W.J.A. (1995) 'Effect of diet on the fatty acid composition of the major phospholipids of infant cerebral cortex', *Archives of Disease in Childhood* **72**, 198–203.

Fedio, P. and Mirsky, A. F. (1969) 'Selective intellectual deficits in children with temporal lobe or centrencephalic epilepsy', *Neuropsychological* **7**, 287–300.

Field, M., Fox, N. and Radcliffe, J. (1990) 'Predicting IQ changes in pre-schoolers with developmental delays', *Developmental and Behavioural Paediatrics* **11**, 184–189.

Filipeck, P.A. (1995) 'Neurobiological correlates of development dyslexia: How do dyslexids' brains differ from those of normal readers?' *Journal of Child Neurology* **10** (supplnt 1), 62–69.

Fletcher, J.M and Satz, P. Filipeck, P.A. (1995) Neurobiological correlates of developmental dyslexia: How do dyslexic's brains differ from those of normal readers? *Journal of Child neurology,* **10** (suppl 1), 62–69 (1983) 'Age plasticity and equipotentiality: a reply to Smith', *Journal of Consulting and Clinical Psychology* **51**, 763–767.

Florey, C. Du V., Leech, A.M., Blackhall, A. (1995) 'Infant feeding and mental and motor development at 18 months of age in first born singletons', *International Journal Epidemiology* **24**, S21–26.

Fog, E. and Fog, M. (1963) 'Cerebral inhibition examined by associated movements', in Bax, M. and Makeith, R. (eds) *Minimal Cerebral Dysfunction. Clinics in Developmental Medicine No. 10.* London: SIMP/Heinemann.

Fox, A.M. and Ho, H. (1990) 'Use of methylphenidate for attention deficit hyperactivity disorder: Canadian Paediatric Society Statement', *Canadian Medical Association Journal* **142**(8), 817–818.

Frostig, M. (1964) *Developmental Test of Visual Perception.* Palo Alto, CA: Consulting Psychological Press.

Gilberg, I.C., Gilberg, C., Groth, J. (1989) 'Children with preschool minor neurodevelopmental disorders v. neurodevelopmental profiles at age 13', *Developmental Medicine and Child Neurology* **31**, 14–24.

Gordon, N., and McKinlay, I. (1980) *Helping Clumsy Children.* New York: Churchill Livingstone.

Greene, R.W. and Barkley, R.A. (1995) 'Clinic-based assessment of attention-deficit/hyperactivity disorder', *Journal of Psychoeducational Assessment, ADHD Monograph Series* 42–60.

Grodzinsky, G. (1990) *Assessing Frontal Lobe Functioning in 6 to 11 year old boys with Attention Deficit Hyperactivity Disorder.* Boston College MA.

Gubbay, S.S. (1975) 'Clumsy children in normal schools', *Medical Journal of Australia* **1**, 223–236.

Gubbay, S.S. (1985) 'Clumsiness', in Vinken, P., Bruyn, G., Dlawans, H. (eds) *Handbook of Clinical Neurology.* New York: Elsevier.

Hack, M. *et al.* (1992) 'The effect of a very low birth weight and social risk on neurocognitive abilities at school age', *Journal Development Behaviour Paediatrics* **13**, 412–420.

Harnadek, M.C.S. and Rourke, B.P. (1994) 'Principal identifying features of the syndrome of nonverbal learning disabilities in children', *Journal of Learning Disability* **27**, 144–154.

Hartsough, C.S. and Lambert, N.M (1985). 'Medical factors in hyperactive and normal children: Prenatal, developmental and health history findings', *American Journal of Orthopsychiatry* **55,** 190–210

Hécaen, H. and Marcie, P. (1974) 'Disorders of written language following right hemisphere lesions', in Dimond, S.J. and Beaumont, J.G. (eds) *Hemisphere Function in the Human Brain.* London: Elek.

Hellgren, L. *et al.* (1994) 'Children with deficits in attention, motor control and perception (DAMP) almost grown up: Psychiatric and personality disorders at age 16 years', *Journal of Child Psychology and Psychiatry* **35**(7), 1255–1271.

Henderson, S.A. (1998) 'Parents and Teachers Guide to Specific Learning Difficulties (dyslexia), Newcastle Upon Tyne: G.T. Harvey and Partners.

Henderson, S.E. (1993) 'Motor development and minor handicap', in Kalverboer, A.E., Hopkins, B., Geuze, R. (eds) *Motor Development in Early and Later Childhood: Longitudinal Approaches.* Cambridge: Cambridge University Press.

Henderson, S.E. and Hall, D. (1982) 'Concomitants of clumsiness in young school children', *Developmental Medicine and Child Neurology* **24,** 448–460.

Henderson, S.E. and Sugden, D. (1992) *Movement Assessment Battery for Children.* New York: Harcourt Brace/The Psychological Corporation.

Hoffman, D.R. *et al.* (1993) 'Effects of supplementation with omega-3 long-chain polyunsaturated fatty acids on retinal and cortical development in premature infants', *American Journal Clinical Nutrition* **58,** 35–42.

Humphries, T. and Bone, J. (1993) 'Use of IQ criteria of evaluating the uniqueness of the learning disability profile', *Journal of Learning Disabilities* **26,** 348–351.

Hynd, G.W. and Cohen, M.J. (1983) *Dyslexia.* New York: Grune and Stratton.

Joschko, M. and Rourke, B.P. (1985) 'Neuropsychological subtypes of learning-disabled children who exhibit the ACID pattern on the WISC', in Rourke, B.P. (ed.) *Neuropsychology of Learning Disabilities: Essentials of Subtype Analysis.* New York: Guilford Press.

Kamhi, A.G (1992) 'Response to historical perspective: a developmental language perspective', *Journal of Learning Disabilities* **25,** 48–52.

Kamphaus, R.W., Benson, J., Hutchinson, S., Platt, L.O. (1994) 'Identification of factor models for the WISC-III', *Educational and Psychological Measurement* **54,** 174–186.

Kaplan, E., Fein, D., Morris, R., Delis, D. (1991) *Manual for WAIS-R as a Neuropsychological Instrument.* San Antonio, TX: The Psychological Corporation.

Kaufman, A. S. (1994) *Intelligence testing with the WISC-III.* New York: A Wiley-Interscience Publication.

Kaufman, A. S. and Kaufman, N. L. (1983) *Kaufman Assessment Battery for Children (K-ABC): Administration and Scoring Manual.* Circle Pines, MN: American Guidance Services.

Keller, E. and Gopnik, M. (eds) (1987) *Motor and Sensory Processes of Language.* Hillsdale, NJ: Lawrence Erlbaum Associates.

Kimbourne, M. (1973) 'Minimal brain dysfunction as a neurodevelopmental lag', *Annals of the New York Academy of Sciences* **205,** 263–273.

Kimura, D. and Archibald, Y. (1974) 'Motor functions of the left hemisphere', *Brain* **97,** 333–350.

Klin, A., Sparrow, S.S., Volkmar, F., Cicchetti, D.V. and Rourke, B.P. (1995) 'Asperger syndrome', in B.P. Rourke (ed.) *Syndrome of Nonverbal Learning Disabilities: Neurodevelopmental manifestations* pp. 93–118. New York: Guilford Press.

Kostura, D.D. (1993) 'Using the WISC-R freedom from distractibility factor to identify attention deficit hyperactivity disorder in children referred for psychoeducational assessment', *Canadian Journal of Special Education* **9,** 91–99.

Lansdell, H. (1969) 'Verbal and non-verbal functions in right-hemisphere speech', *Journal of Comparative and Physiological Psychology*, 734–738.

Lanting, C.I. *et al.* (1994) 'Neurological differences between 9-year-old children fed breast-milk or formula-milk as babies', *Lancet* **344,** 319–322.

Laszlo, J.I. and Bairstow, P.J. (1986) *Perceptual Motor Behaviour.* New York: Holt, Rinehart and Winston.

Lee, M.G and French, J. (1997) *Dyspraxia – a Handbook for Therapists.* Chartered Society of Physiotherapy.

Lee, M.G. and Smith, G.N. (1998) 'The effectiveness of physiotherapy for dyspraxia', *Physiotherapy* **84** (6), 276–284.

Lucas, A. *et al.* (1989). 'Early diet in pre-term babies and developmental status in infancy', *Archives of Disease in Childhood* **64,** 1578.

Lucas, A. *et al.* (1992) 'Breast milk and subsequent intelligence quotient in children born prematurely', *Lancet* **339**, 261–264.

McCormick, L. Schiefelbusch, R.L. (1997) *Supporting Children with Communication Difficulties in Inclusive Settings.* Boston, MA: Allyn and Bacon.

Maccow, G. and Laurent, J. (1996) 'Analysing WISC-III profiles: A comparison of two approaches', *Journal of Psychoeducational Assessment* **14**, 0–31.

Makrides, M. *et al.* (1995) 'Are long-chain polyunsaturated fatty acids essential nutrients in infancy?' *Lancet* **345**, 1463–1468.

Makrides, M., Neumann, M.A., Byard, R.W., Simmer, K., Gibson, R.A. (1994) 'Fatty acid composition of brain, retina and erythrocytes in breast- and formula-fed infants', *American Journal Clinical Nutrition* **60**, 189–194.

Makrides, M., Neumann, M.A., Gibson, R.A. (1996) 'Effect of maternal docosahexanoic acid (DHA) supplementation on breast milk composition', *European Journal of Clinical Nutrition* **50**, 352–357.

Mattson, A.J., Sheer, D.E. and Fletcher, J.M. (1992) 'Electrophysiological evidence of lateralized disturbances in children with disabilities', *Journal of Clinical and Experimental Neuropsychology* **14**, 707–716.

Milloy, N. (1991) *Breakdown of Speech: Causes and Remediation.* London: Chapman and Hall.

Missiuna, C., Bushby, C., Rupert, C. (1994) *Management of Children with Developmental Co-ordination Disorder: at Home and in the Classroom.* Hamilton, Ontario: Cheryl Missiuna.

Morris, J.M. and Bigler, E.D. (1987) 'Hemispheric functioning and the Kaufman Assessment Battery for Children. Results in the neurologically impaired', *Developmental Neuropsychology* **3**, 67–79.

Nadeau, K. (1995) *Attention Deficit Hyperactivity Disorder in Adults: A Handbook.* New York: Brunner/Mazel.

Neuringer, M. *et al.* (1988) 'The essentiality of n-3 fatty acids for the development and function of the retina and brain', *Annual Review of Nutrition* **8**, 517–541.

Neuringer, M. (1993) 'Cerebral cortex docosahexanoic acid is lower in formula-fed than in breast-fed infants', *Nutrition Review* **51**, 238–241.

Newby, R.F., Recht, D.R., Caldwell, J. and Schaefer, J. (1993) 'Comparison of WISC-III and WISC-R IQ changes over a 2-year time span in a sample of children with dyslexia', in B.A. Bracken & R.S. McCallum (eds) *Journal of Psychoeducational Assessment, WISC-III Monograph,* 87–93.

Ozols, E.J. and Rourke, B.P. (1988) 'Characteristics of young children with learning disabilities classified according to patterns of academic achievement: auditory-perceptual and visual-perceptual disabilities', *Journal of Clinical Child Psychology* **17**, 44–52.

Ozonoff, S. *et al.* (1994) 'Executive function abilities in autism and tourette syndrome: an information processing approach', *Journal of Child Psychology and Psychiatry and Allied Disciplines* **35**(6), 1015–1032.

Petrauskas, R.J. and Rourke B.P. (1979) 'Identification of subtypes of retarded readers: A neuropsychological, multivariate approach', *Journal of Clinical Neuropsychology* **1**, 17–37.

Phelps, L., Leguori, S., Nisewaner, K. and Parker, M. (1993) 'Practical interpretations of the WISC-III with language disordered children', *Journal of Psychoeducational Assessment,* WISC-III Monograph, 71–76.

Polatajko, H.J. *et al.* (1995) 'Clinical trial of the process-orientated treatment approach for children with developmental co-ordination disorder', *Developmental Medicine and Child Neurology* **37**(4), 310–319.

Portwood, M.M. (1996) *Developmental Dyspraxia – a Practical Manual for Parents and Professionals.* Durham LEA.

Portwood, M.M. (1999) *Developmental Dyspraxia – Identification and Intervention.* London: David Fulton Publishers.

Prifitera, A. and Dersh, J. (1993) 'Base rates of WISC-III diagnostic subtest patterns among normal, learning disabled, and ADHD samples', *Journal of Psychoeduational Assessment,* WISC-III Monograph, 43–55.

Prifitera, A. and Saklofske, D. (1998) *WISC III Clinical Use and Interpretation.* New York: Academic Press.

Rauscher, H.H. (1994) 'Music and Spatial Task Performance. A Causal Relationship'. Paper presented to American Psychological Association (August 1994).

Reschly, D.J. (1997) 'Diagnostic and treatment utility of intelligence tests', in Flanagan, J.L., Genshaft, J.L. and Harrison, L. (eds) *Contemporary Intellectual Assessment: Theories, Tests and Issues.* New York: Guilford Press.

Revel, C. (1998) 'Research and development', interim report for the Dyspraxia Foundation Adult Group. Hitchin: The Dyspraxia Foundation.

Rourke, B.P. (1989) *Non-verbal Learning Disabilities: The Syndrome and the Model.* New York: Guilford Press.

Rourke, B.P. (ed.) (1995) *Syndrome of Non-verbal Learning Disabilities: Neurodevelopmental Manifestations.* New York: Guilford Press.

Rourke, B.P., Dietrich, D.M. and Young, G.C. (1973) 'Significance of WISC verbal-performance discrepancies for younger children with learning disabilities', *Perceptual and Motor Skills* **36**, 275–282.

Rourke, B.P., Fisk, J.L. and Strang, J.D. (1986) *Neuropsychological Assessment of Children: A Treatment-orientated Approach*. New York: Guilford.

Rourke, B.P. and Fisk, J.L. (1988) 'Subtypes of learning-disabled children: Implications for a neurodevelopmental model of differential hemispheric processing', in Molfese, D.L. and Segalowitz, S.J. (eds) *Brain Lateralisation in Children: Developmental Implications* (pp. 547–565). New York: Guilford Press.

Rourke, B.P., Young, G.C. and Flewelling, R.W. (1971) 'The relationship between WISC verbal performance discrepancies and selective verbal, auditory-perceptual, visual-perceptual, and problem solving abilities in children with learning disabilities', *Journal of Clinical Psychology* **27**, 465–479.

Rovet, J. (1995) 'Congenital hypothyroidism', in Rourke, B.P. (ed.) *Syndrome of Non-Verbal Learning Disabilities: Manifestations in Neurological Disease, Disorder and Dysfunction*. New York: Guilford Press.

Rudel, R.G. and Denckla, M.B. (1974) 'Relationship of forward and backward digit repetitions to neurological impairment in children with learning disabilities', *Neuropsychologia* **12**, 109–118.

Russell, J. (1988) *Graded Activities for Children with Motor Difficulties*. Cambridge: Cambridge University Press.

Russel, P. (1997) *The Brain Book*. London: Routledge.

Saffran, E.M. (1982) 'Neuropsychological approaches to the study of language', *British Journal of Psychology* **73**, 317–337.

Saklofske, D.H. and Schwean, V.L. (1993) 'Standardised procedures for measuring the correlates of ADHD in children: A research program', *Canadian Journal of School Psychology* **9**, 28–36.

Searleman, A. (1983) 'Language capabilities of the right hemisphere', in Young, A.W. (ed.) *Functions of the Right Cerebral Hemisphere*. London: Academic Press.

Seidman, L.J. *et al.* (1995) 'Effects of family history and comorbidity on the neuropsychological performance of children with ADHD: preliminary findings', *Journal of the American Academy of Child and Adolescent Psychiatry* **34**, 1015–1024.

Shaffer, D. *et al.* (1993) 'Neurological soft signs: their relationship to psychiatric disorder and intelligence in childhood and adolescence', *Archives of General Psychiatry* **42**, 342–351.

Shattock, P. and Savery, D. (1996) *Urinary Profiles of People with Autism: Possible Implications and Relevance to other Research*, Autism Research Unit, University of Sunderland.

Shattock, P. and Savery, D. (1997) '*Evaluation of Urinary Profiles Obtained from People with Autism and Associated Disorders. Classification of Subgroups*' Autism Research Unit,University of Sunderland.

Shaywitz, S.E. and Shaywitz, B.A (1984) 'Diagnosis and management of Attention Deficit Disorder: a paediatric perspective', *Paediatric Clinics of North America* **31**, 429–457.

Shreibman, L. (1988) *Autism*. Newbury Park, CA: Sage.

Stevens, L.J. *et al.* (1995) 'Essential fatty acid metabolism in boys with attention-deficit hyperactivity disorder', *American Journal Clinical Nutrition* **62,** 761–768.

Szatmari, P., Offord, D.R. and Boyle, M.H. (1989a) 'Prevalence of attention deficit disorder with hyperactivity', *Journal of Child Psychology and Psychiatry* **30,** 219–230.

Szatmari, P., Offord, D.R. and Boyle, M.H. (1989b) 'Correlates, associated impairments and patterns of service utilisation of children with attention deficit disorders: Findings from the Ontario child health study', *Journal of Child Psychology and Psychiatry* **30,** 205–217.

Talay-Ongan, A. (1998) *Typical and Atypical Development in Early Childhood. The Fundamentals.* Leicester: British Psychological Society.

Talay-Senkal, A. (1978) 'Development of asymmetry of brain function for language activity in children as reflected by performance on a listening and viewing task', Hacettepe University *Bulletin of Social Sciences* **11,** 135–147.

Teodorescu, I. and Addy, L. (1998) *Write from the Start.* Cambridge: L.D.A.

Thelen, E. (1989) 'The (re)discovery of motor development: Learning new things from an old field', *Developmental Psychology* **25,** 946–949.

van der Vlugt, H. (1991) 'Neuropsychological validation studies of learning disabilities subtypes: Verbal, visual-spatial, and psychomotor abilities', in Rourke, B.P. (ed.) *Neuropsychological Validation of Learning Disability Subtypes* (pp. 140–159). New York: Guilford Press.

Wechsler, D. (1991) *Manual for the Wechsler Intelligence Scale for Children. Third Edition.* New York: The Psychological Corporation.

Wechsler, D. (1992) *WPPSI-R. UK., WISC-III, WAIS.* New York: The Psychological Corporation/Harcourt, Brace.

Wechsler, D. (1996) *Wechsler Objective Reading Dimensions (WORD).* New York: The Psychological Corporation/Harcourt, Brace.

Wender, P.H. (1971) *Minimal Brain Dysfunction in Children.* New York: Wiley.

Wetton, P. (1997) *Physical Education in the Early Years.* London: Routledge.

White, M., Bungay, C., Gabriel, H. (1994) *Guide to Early Movement Skills.* Slough: NFER-Nelson.

Williams, L.V. (1983) *Teaching for the Two-Sided Mind.* New York: Simon and Schuster.

Zentall, S.S. (1988) 'Production deficiencies in elicited language but not in the spontaneous verbalisation of hyperactive children', *Journal of Abnormal Child Psychology* **16,** 657–673.

Index